WE'VE DONE
THEM WRONG!

WE'VE DONE THEM WRONG!

A History of the Native American Indians and How the United States Treated Them

By George E. Saurman

iUniverse, Inc.
Bloomington

We've Done Them Wrong!
A History of the Native American Indians and How the United States Treated Them

iUniverse books may be ordered through booksellers or by contacting:

iUniverse
1663 Liberty Drive
Bloomington, IN 47403
www.iuniverse.com
1-800-Authors (1-800-288-4677)

ISBN: 978-1-4759-4488-4 (sc)
ISBN: 978-1-4759-4490-7 (hc)
ISBN: 978-1-4759-4489-1 (ebk)

Library of Congress Control Number: 2012915676

Printed in the United States of America

iUniverse rev. date: 08/23/2012

Contents

Acknowledgement

It is with a great deal of gratitude that I acknowledge the valuable assistance of Jeffrey Fehlenberg who critiqued my work early on and made me aware that I was guilty of approaching much of my evaluation from the white man's point of view. His great understanding of the Native American Indian culture enabled me to more evenly balance my presentation. In spite of the very disturbing treatment of these first citizens by our ancestors, I wanted to strike a sense of understanding from the point of view of both sides in the development of a new nation.

Introduction

This book is intended to be an apologetic admission of gross transgressions of the United States against the inhabitants of this land when the "civilization" of Western Europe entered the New World in the name of colonization, and which unfortunately, continue even today. As a nation we have defeated greedy anarchies, power hungry dictators, potential invaders in many parts of the world, and in every case we have rebuilt what we destroyed. In our dealings with the Native American Indians, however, we have been less than fair, certainly not compassionate, and in many instances cruel and downright dishonest.

This book can be summarized best by remarks made by Kevin Gover, Assistant Secretary of Indian Affairs in the Department of Interior Affairs at a ceremony celebrating the 175th Anniversary of the establishment of the Bureau of Indian Affairs in the Department of the Interior, delivered on September 8, 2000.

"We must first reconcile ourselves to the fact that the works of this agency have at various times profoundly harmed the communities it was meant to serve. From the very beginning the Office of Indian Affairs was an instrument by which the United States enforced its ambition against the Indian nations and Indian people who stood in its path."

He referenced the "Trail of Tears" and described the agency's role in ethnic cleansing citing the deliberate spread of disease, the destruction of huge numbers of buffalo herds and even the use of alcohol to destroy both mind and body. He even acknowledged the killing of women and children which he described as cowardly.

He further spoke of the needless and violent massacres which actions took place at Sand Creek and Wounded Knee. He recognized planned efforts to total annihilate the Indian culture which ultimately led to the destruction of tribal economies and which were intended to render the total dependence of the Indian population on services which the agency he represented was supposed to provide.

The agency proceeded to forbid the speaking of Indian languages, it disallowed traditional religious activities, outlawed traditional government and sought to make Native American Indians ashamed of who they were. He further put the blame for the shameful conduct of the boarding schools for the children on the Bureau of Indian Affairs, describing the conduct employed as "brutalizing them emotionally, psychologically, physically and spiritually."

While he sought to present the present conduct of the Bureau as finally serving the people it was supposed to protect all along, he acknowledges the legacy which the past has thrust upon them. He refers to the passing of the trauma of shame, fear and anger of the past from one generation to another and admits that past events have resulted in wide spread alcoholism, drug abuse and domestic violence taking place on today's reservations.

He summarizes that many of the difficulties found today in Indian country are the result of the mistreatment suffered throughout our history as our nation grew and moved across the country. He states that poverty, ignorance and disease have been the by-products of the past conduct of the agency.

He confesses that in the past the agency has committed acts so terrible that they continue to infect, diminish and destroy the lives of Indian people still today.

And he also vows that these wrongs must be acknowledged if the healing is to take place. He concludes with a call to wipe away the tears of seven generations and allow broken hearts to mend.

"The Bureau of Indian Affairs was born in 1824 in a time of war on Indian people. May it live in the year 2000 and beyond as an instrument of their prosperity," said the Assistant Secretary.

Politically these words sound good. They do enumerate some of the transgressions which took place, but like the bureau itself which was publicized as an agency intended to protect and assist the Native American Indians, it was and remains, a weapon by which the government continues to wrest additional lands and rights from the original inhabitants of America.

Once again, whether the people of the agency failed the red man in preventing the devastation or whether indeed they performed well their real mission to make it happen is a matter for debate.

While the Assistant Secretary of Indian Affairs is most certainly aware of what happened at Sand Creek and Wounded Knee, most people haven't a clue. You will read the details of these massacres and others later in this book, but it is unlikely that without fully understanding the immensity of these travesties, one would be less likely to understand the true impact of the needless killing involved.

It is helpful to realize that his reference to tribal economies should include intertribal economies as well. As the Europeans brought metal tools, shiny beads, colorful fabrics and firearms they began to displace intertribal commerce that had been fruitful for many generations. Many trade routes existed on land and over waterways not only between villages, but also between different tribes. Trade language used at the time still exists.

In outlawing traditional governments the federal government sought to establish governments within the Native population that were more convenient for them to deal with. Our concept of "chiefs" gives far more power to them than actually existed. The chief was a facilitator and leader by example. Decisions were made communally which created an environment with which it was difficult for the colonists to deal. There was no one person with whom they could negotiate and they wanted to change that.

Justice for the American Native Indian is still unfortunately very elusive. In April of 2008, the Colorado Legislature passed a resolution comparing the deaths of millions of Native American Indians to the Holocaust.

On December 4, 2009, a headline in the Intelligencer, a local Pennsylvania newspaper read, "IRS Sells Indian Tribe's Land to Settle Debt." The article goes on to describe that 7,100 acres, a total of eleven square miles of Crow Creek Sioux tribal land in central South Dakota was auctioned off for 2.6 million dollars which was less than its appraised value of 4.6 million dollars to pay for federal employment taxes owed by the tribe.

The tribe had previously been told by the Office of Indian Affairs that federally recognized tribes did not have to pay these taxes. The land was part of the tribe's original reservation established in an 1868 treaty. The tribe filed a lawsuit on December 7 seeking to block the sale. Judge Roberto A. Lange declined their request, but promised to schedule a trial to hear the tribe's arguments. At the time of this writing there has been no decision.

What I have attempted to do in this book is to point out some of the facts surrounding the building of one great nation, while at the same time destroying many others. My intention, however, is not to condemn, but rather to hopefully help others recognize the great debt that we owe to these people and to encourage every effort to make amends and move forward together. We must never again allow such atrocities to occur or such discrimination to continue to exist.

In conversations with other people, I have found that most are unaware of many of the events that transpired with regard to the official treatment of the Native American Indians. It has either been lost in the maze of other activities or purposely hidden from the American public, but certainly not found in our American history books. And while illegal immigrants carry the day in today's media reports, somehow the original inhabitants of this great land are unreported and seemingly remain an inconvenience to the American conscience.

I was aware of the help that the Indians had given to the colonists in Massachusetts and their role in the first Thanksgiving. I was also aware of their participation in the settling of Jamestown, Virginia. However, their subsequent contributions as veterans in every war that we have been involved in and especially the role of the Navajo Code Talkers in World War II have received far less recognition than they deserve, even though President Ronald Reagan declared August 14th as National Navajo Code Talkers Day.

The absence of any mention of the contributions of the Iroquois Confederacy to the establishment of our form of government is embarrassing. I will explain more of that later. Their described role in our history has been that of a constant enemy and a threat to the lives of the invading settlers. Their contributions have been all but ignored.

Only recently has the realization of the plight of the American Indian really hit home for me. It began with a small response to a request for money from the former Olympic champion and U.S Marine Officer, Billy Mills, who has dedicated his life to helping his fellow natives with a program called, "Running Strong for American Indian Youth."

Since then I have been contacted by several groups, all describing the extreme conditions of poverty existing on their respective reservations and seeking assistance. In spite of our great verbal dedication to justice, we have banished them to the most difficult areas of this continent where they must try to survive. On many reservations they face a shortage of water, poor soil, extremes of temperature and weather conditions that constantly challenge their very existence.

While we expend billions of dollars in aid to third world countries annually, the amount budgeted for aid to Native Americans is pitiful by comparison and the effort to establish a situation which lends itself to humane potential is simply not being adequately addressed.

It was because of this personal awakening that I determined to thoroughly research the situation and share my findings with others in the hope that it might ignite a search for a remedial solution and in the meantime encourage as many individuals as possible to support the charitable organizations listed at the end of the book that are attempting to provide some of the daily needs of life for these impoverished Native elders and children seeking survival in a cruel and unyielding environment.

The contents of this book represent several hundreds of hours of reading and study which have caused me to become passionate in the desire to pierce the silence which has surrounded this inconvenient inheritance left to us by our forefathers. We are a great Nation and have an obligation to do much better than we have done to date.

Chapter One

The New World before the Invaders

History has described the continents of North and South America as the "New World" as it related to the then known world of Europe and Asia. There was even the incorrect assumption on the part of early geographers, that if you traveled far enough west on this flat surface called earth, you would fall off. Maps didn't include the continent of North America, because it had not yet been "discovered" by the European adventurers.

However, the continent did exist, having been included as part of creation. Not only did it exist, but it was inhabited. According to anthropologists, the first inhabitants of the Americas migrated across the Bering Strait to Alaska by way of existing land bridges, probably in search of game. They resembled the early Mongoloid people of northeastern Asia, with medium skin pigmentation. For the most part, their hair was black and straight, with minimal body hair and very little balding. However, they have several unique characteristics which distinguish them from the Mongoloids.

Estimates vary as to the total number which existed before the coming of the Europeans, but it runs as high as eighteen million. And the time table for their migration is nowhere recorded, but it is believed to have been 20,000 to 30,000 years ago and it is obvious that once they crossed onto this continent, they spread out, going both south and east, breaking into many hundreds of different nations and tribes.

The Walum Olum (Red Score) is reportedly a historical narrative of the Lenape (Delaware) Indians. Botanist and antiquarian Constantine Samuel Rafinesque published an account in 1830 which he claimed

1

to have been an English translation of the original story as told by the Indians. It suggests a migration some 3600 years before his writing and while its authenticity has been questioned, it is the position of the Lenape Nation of Pennsylvania that they have been in the area for 10,000 years.

The Indians were adaptable and wherever they wound up they made wise use of the natural resources available to them. They respected the land and all that it had to offer. Different conditions caused them to live in different ways. When they found good hunting and an adequate supply of berries and seeds, they settled down and learned to utilize the trees and plants, as well as the animals, fish, birds and even the stones and land itself for their sustenance.

They were the first to grow potatoes, tomatoes and many other food staples that continue to provide nourishment for people throughout the world today. They were the first to raise turkeys. They found uses for Native American products such as rubber, tobacco and sugar maple and even utilized the cinchona tree, the source of quinine.

Because of the vast variation in climate and the kinds of land involved, the various Indian tribes reflected these differences in their clothing, food, shelter and even the way they lived. Since they depended on nature, they studied the animals, determined which plants were poisonous and which were good for eating. They even identified plants that were good for medicine. And they learned the signs of weather variations and even the changing seasons.

With no text books to explain nature they believed the sun, rain, wind and other forces of nature were controlled by spirits and they worshipped animals, plants, the sun, rain and wind in ceremonies and prayers by which they sought to gain favor with these deities in accordance with the teachings of earlier generations.

Scholars explain culture as the way of life of a people. They have identified several cultures in the pre-European North American arena. Because the inhabitants shared many of the same environmental factors, they shared much of the same culture.

Because there was no technical system of immediate communication, the Indians developed many ways to send signals, such as waving buffalo robes, marking trails, audible signals which were made by drums, horns and shells, or by using smoke signals by day and fire by night. To communicate most information they depended upon storytellers to travel from one band or tribe to the next, carrying the message.

These traveling storytellers had free passage through foreign territories in Indian lands and they carried news of births and deaths, wars and treaties. Each storyteller was held in high esteem for his or her role in tribal life. The tradition carries on today and storytellers are still considered very important tribal members. Such people existed in Europe before newspapers appeared which eventually replaced them.

Eastern Indians

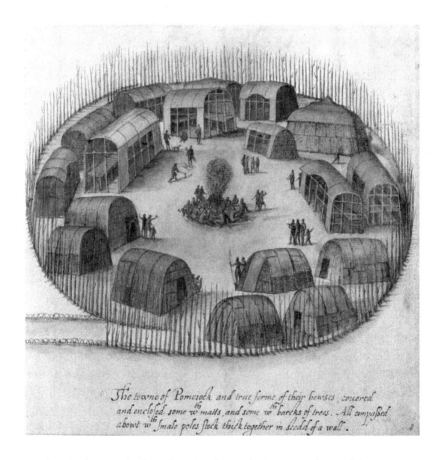

The towne of Pomeiock and true forme of their howses, couered and enclosed some wth matts, and some wth barcks of trees. All compassed abowt wth smale poles stock thick together in stedd of a wall.

Those who made their homes along the Eastern part of the continent enjoyed a climate with much rainfall. Forests spread out to cover both the mountains and the valleys. Lakes and streams were also found in abundance. The inhabitants depended upon the trees, the animals that dwelt in the woods and the fish and shellfish that were plentiful in the streams and ocean for food.

They selected tree bark and branches to provide shelter and also many of their weapons and utensils. Hollowed trees provided canoes for traveling over the waters. Most of their clothing came from the skin of animals. Because they knew how to grow crops and because game was plentiful, they could live in villages. The women planted corn, pumpkin, squash, beans, tobacco and gourds. Usually the weather was cooperative, especially in the warm, rainy summers.

The village was a busy place. The men helped with building wigwams and they made areas for gardens by burning off the trees and bushes. Trees were cut by a method called girdling. Wet clay was located a short distance up the trunk and then a fire started at the base. Then the fire was extinguished and the Indian would use a primitive stone axe to chip away until the tree fell. Lack of sharp tools was a major hindrance to the Indians. Skilled men of the tribe made bows and arrows, war clubs and stone knives from bones and wood from trees and bushes in addition to the stones they found in abundance on the ground.

Many chores kept the women busy most of the day. They wrapped the babies in moss and furs and bound them in wooden cradleboards. These they carried on their backs while gathering food. While in the village they stood the boards by the house and while working in the garden simply hung the cradleboard on a tree limb.

It was their responsibility to plant the seeds in the garden and harvest the food when ready. They also prepared the meals. One method was to roast green corn in a pit with hot rocks or to broil meat or fish on a grill of green twigs over a fire.

To grind dry corn they had to pound it in a mortar made of a hollowed log with a small piece of wood for a pestle. To make hominy they soaked grains in a solution of wood ashes to loosen the hull of the kernel. They parched or toasted corn for warriors on the march. In addition they dried vegetables, fish and meat for the winter months. Pottery jars were used in which to stew foods.

Many days were required to make their buckskin clothing. The tanning of deer hides involved many steps. The flesh had to be scraped from the hide along with the hair then the hide was washed, dried and stretched. Sometimes they smoked it to make it waterproof.

Shell or flint knives were used cut the skins to make it fit and then they were sewn with sinew from animals. Awls and needles were made from bones or horns. The women decorated clothing with beautiful porcupine embroidery, colored or stained hides, and used shells, wampum, colorful stones or rocks, bones and plant matter to enhance the appearance of clothing. The ability of the Indians to utilize what nature provided was amazing.

The Plains Indians

The Plains Indians lived on the rolling terrain of the mid-west where there was sufficient rain to maintain a thick carpet of grass, but not enough to grow many trees, most of which bordered the rivers. Huge herds of grazing animals found the grass to their liking.

Foremost among these animals was the buffalo or bison which came to be considered by some as "the Plains Indian's galloping department store" because it provided them with most of the things that they needed. They ate the flesh and made tents from the skin, which were called teepees. The word "tipi" in the Siouan language refers to a dwelling place. It could refer to a Hogan, a tent, a lean-to, or a modern home. The tents made from buffalo skins were mostly sharp pointed, although larger tents were elongated in order to accommodate more people.

Skins were also used to make boats, utensils, baggage and some items of clothing. Bones were used to make utensils and even the stomach was used to form a cooking utensil by lining a hole in the ground.

Hunting was usually a tribal activity, especially in the case of the buffalo. Over the centuries the hunters had developed strategies to reap the desired number of buffalo. If the herd was scattered, a few of them would move quietly among the animals and shoot several with their arrows.

A more successful plan was to station one man draped in a buffalo robe at the edge of a cliff. The other Indians would circle behind the animals and jump up from behind the herd, shouting and waving robes. The buffalo would begin to trot, then gallop in the direction of the decoy. The animals in the rear would push those in front. The decoy Indian would jump aside and the buffalo would go over the cliff where many were killed and the others shot with bow and arrow.

After the hunt there was much to be done. The animals had to be skinned and the meat hung over a fire on green branches to cook, or perhaps cut up, and put in a pot to boil. The buffalo even provided the pot which was made from the stomach or a piece of hide fitted into a hole in the ground. Hot rocks were dropped into the pot to do the boiling.

The Plains Indians moved on foot about the open lands following the herds. They also hunted other animals found in the area such as elk, deer and antelope. In order to transport their small portable shelters, dogs were employed.

The introduction of horses in the 1500s by the Spaniards brought about many cultural changes, transforming them from plodding pedestrians to nomadic hunters and warriors. Once they were able to utilize this "Big Dog," life took on a different complexion.

They became famous as expert hunters. With their swift ponies they could easily overtake a herd of buffalo and kill all the animals they needed. Horse stealing between tribes became a big sporting event and an honorable way for a young warrior to achieve a reputation for himself.

Horses became an integral part of a horse medicine cult featuring a dance in imitation of horses, which was believed to influence the outcome of horse races, heal sick horses, calm a particularly wild horse and even affect the quality of a newborn horse.

Ornaments and war paint had special meaning to the Plains Indians and was not intended for cosmetic reasons. They painted their bodies for dances and for battle. After smearing their bodies with a base coat of buffalo or deer fat, they used red and white clays, black charcoal and yellow pigment from bull berries or moss for paint.

The practice of using animal grease or fish oil to clean and soften the skin was common among Indians even though it resulted in an unpleasant odor. They also practiced the use of a sweat bath. For this purpose they constructed an airtight hut in which they placed hot stones. Called an inipi, the process is a ceremony by which the individual's soul and conscience is cleansed. By sprinkling water on the stones they created steam. The Indian would stay inside the hut until perspiring freely and then dash outside and jump into a cold stream of water.

Pueblo Indians of the Southwest

The Indians of the Southwest lived on land that was high and dry. It was divided by mountains and canyons. Rain was sparse but came in the summer when it did the most good for the crops. Snow fell on the mountains in the winter and supplied water for streams, springs and watering holes, The Pueblo Indians learned how to irrigate and find moist locations for farming. Good crops provided adequate food for the most part.

Early Pueblo Indians carved homes in canyon walls or inhabited existing caves. Later, they built large homes from stone and adobe (sun-dried clay) in which whole villages lived. These buildings had several stories and many rooms. The ground floor was constructed without doors or windows. The second floor was built leaving the space of a room which provided a kind of front porch for the inhabitants. If there was another floor, the same arrangement provided another front porch. Each level was reached by means of a ladder. People often watched dances held in a common area outside the residences from these "front lawn" locations.

The name "Pueblo" was them given by the Spaniards because of their communities. The most important focus of these Pueblo Indians was, and remains, the "kiva" which is a stone-walled ceremonial and meeting chamber, usually dug deep into the ground somewhere prominently in the village. These units symbolize the World Below and are the domain of the spirits which inhabit all creation.

Of special significance is the "sipapu," a stone-lined hole in the floor of the kiva, which is a passage way for the spirits. It is also this World Below to which the Hopi Indians believe they will return after death. The Hopi Pueblo village at Oraibi, Arizona, is one of the two oldest continuously occupied settlements on the North American continent north of Mexico.

Oraibi was located on top of the mesa and to reach the area where they planted and hunted, the men had to descend more than 600 feet of steep cliff, along trails that were cut into crevices. Once down, they often had to travel a great distance to where their crops were planted.

Although often thought of as one people, the Pueblo Indians were divided into many tribes with four different languages. Farthest west were the Hopi villages located on high, flat surfaces called mesas. They were located where springs could be found. Across the border, in what is now New Mexico, were the Zunis. These two groups made up what was referred to as the dessert Pueblos. Along the Rio Grande River, as it flowed through New Mexico, were the river Pueblos.

Pueblo farmers knew how to locate underground water by studying the growth of wild plants. They then located their fields where there would be moisture for the crops to grow. This sometimes resulted in a field located at a distance from their shelter.

Among the Pueblo Indians the man was the farmer. He did so with primitive tools. A tough but sharp digging stick was driven into the ground to a distance of about eighteen inches. He would drop in a host of kernels so that some would grow. The seeds sent their roots deep into the ground and the stalks grew in clumps. The farmer then created dams with branches to direct the water to the plants. Sometimes he would dig a ditch from a stream to the area of his crops to irrigate.

There is a legend of Three Sisters involving corn, beans and squash. The Indians believed that each had its own spirit in the form of three sisters who were very fond of each other and enjoyed living together. They were planted together to provide physical protection and nutritional abundance.

Corn is the eldest and was planted first. When it reached about four inches in height, the beans were planted. As the corn grew tall, reaching for the sun, the bean grew up the corn. A week after the bean sprouted, the squash was planted. It grew over the ground, protecting her sisters from weeds and keeping the ground moist.

When it was time to harvest the corn there was a great celebration. The corn was spread out on the flat roofs to dry. Strips of squash were hung on branches to dry and the women pounded dry beans with sticks to open the pods and then they emptied the contents into a basket. It was a regular practice to store about two year's supply of their crops to provide for a lean year.

When marrying there was a strict prohibition of the two partners coming from the same clan. Mating with someone in the same maternal line of descent was sacrilege. Once a marriage was agreed to, the boy and girl had their hair washed in the same basin, a ceremony symbolizing the mingling of their lives.

The groom-to-be worked to weave a marriage costume for his bride. He spun cotton into cloth and then wove it into two blankets and a white-fringed belt. He also made her a set of white leggings and a pair of white moccasins. When finished, the two moved from the

9

groom's house to that of the bride where they would remain for the rest of their lives.

In other geographic areas the Pima and Papago tribes, located in what later became southern Arizona, lived in simple huts made from a framework of logs and poles which were covered with arrow wood or grass and held together with clay.

While closely related, the two tribes shared different homelands and hence had somewhat different lifestyles. The Pima were located along the Salt and Gila Rivers in an area that was environmentally friendlier than the arid dessert where the Papago lived. The Pima could establish villages, but the Papago lived as nomads. They lived in "field villages" in the desert during the summers where heavy rains provided the necessary water. In the winter, they had to retreat to their "well villages" located near springs, where they depended mostly on stored foods and hunting for sustenance.

In the northern territory, the Navajo and Apache Indians were hunters who raided the villages. They didn't settle in villages, but were nomadic, following game and attacking other tribes when game was scarce. After the influx of the Spaniards, with the introduction of sheep and goats, they raided the Spanish settlers and stole sheep, but instead of eating them, they kept them to build herds of their own. After they began herding sheep themselves, they were forced to move over the dry, rocky land seeking grass for their flocks.

At this point they built homes from stones, logs and earth called hogans. Because of the need to move in search of grazing according to the seasons, they had summer and winter homes, following the same routes as they moved about.

Within the Navajo society, women played a pivotal role, as in most Indian culture. Possessions were passed from mother to daughter. When married, the man moved in with his wife's family. Oddly, he continued to have responsibilities to his mother and sisters which would at times cause him to be absent from his own wife and children.

Unlike the Navajo, the Apaches never settled into farming or herding sheep. Instead they continued an existence supported mainly by raiding the various Pueblo tribes that lived nearby and hunting the animals that roamed about in the fields and forests. They lived in "wickiups," hut-like structures made of slender poles, covered with brush and grass.

Apache women did little with pottery, but were skilled in making baskets which were used for many things, such as cooking and storing food.

The Seed Gatherers

Another culture was known as the Seed Gatherers. They lived in an even drier environment found mostly in the arid parts of California and in the Great Basin between the Rockies and the Sierra Nevada. They were often unable to find adequate game so the men roamed the dessert while the women gathered berries, nuts, seeds and roots, grinding the seeds into flour from which they made gruel. Much of their life was spent in wandering from one oasis to another searching for water, firewood and food.

Again, because of their environment, their shelters were flimsy huts which kept out the wind. They were covered with rushes or clusters of grass to keep out the rain. Often they dug a pit about two feet deep under the shelter. This was easier than building walls and kept drafts out. During the winters they camped in a sheltered valley and ate dried foods. They heaped mounds of dirt over the shelter to keep the cold out.

When the temperature allowed, both the men and children were usually naked. The women made fringed aprons out of the fibers of sagebrush bark, milkweed or Indian hemp.

During colder weather the men used pelts to wrap around their shoulders or, if lucky, they could fasten a couple of skins together with thong. Older men used strips of rabbit skin woven into a blanket.

Tattoo designs were common for both men and women. Stripes on the chin were considered special for the women. Special marks were tattooed on the chins of young girls as a sign of maturity. Bones, hooves of deer, berries and shells from the sea provided ornaments and were often made into necklaces.

Yucca fiber was made into thick sandals. If animal hides were available they were made into moccasins. The jack rabbit was a particular prize, because of the many uses for its fur as well as the meat for food. However, it required 100 skins to make a man's robe for winter wear and 40 for a child's coat.

Because they were constantly moving about they utilized baskets, rather than pottery. Baskets were lighter and less likely to break as they were moved about. The natives were able to weave them so tightly that they were able to hold water and could be used in cooking.

Preparation of food was a difficult task. They had to crack acorns and remove the kernels, then pound them into meal which had to be washed in hot water to remove the poisonous tannin. Even tiny seeds from flowering plants were beaten into flour. The women then made gruel and cooked it by dropping hot rocks into water in one of their baskets. The resulting product could be eaten by hand. Sixty different plants have been identified as having been eaten.

Sometimes they ate crickets, insect larvae, grasshoppers and ants which were ground into flour. Certain lizards and snakes were eaten when game was scarce, which it often was, along with pack rats and ground squirrels and mice.

Indians of California

It seemed that everything the Great Basin lacked, western California provided. The rain, which was so rare on the eastern slopes, fell generously on the western slopes and the Native Indians existed in large numbers. The Mohave, found along the Colorado River Valley, were among the tallest humans on the continent.

There were more than a hundred different dialects spoken by the inhabitants, but in spite of their language differences they shared a great many more things in common. They ate many of the same foods, lived in similar homes and wore similar types of clothing.

Migratory salmon was the staple food although deer, elk and smaller game were also a part of the regular diet because of their availability. Homes were for the most part single family, accommodating six or seven individuals. About a hundred gathered to form a loosely constructed village.

California Indians seldom engaged in warfare. With food in abundance and no strong tribal association, conflict was usually a matter of individual differences which could be resolved without resort to force.

In the Santa Barbara Bay area, the Chumash learned to take advantage of ocean fishing and so were able to provide abundantly for themselves when the weather was warmer. They found adequate hunting of deer and smaller game, combined with an abundance of acorns from oak trees, as the weather turned colder.

Chumash Indians fished from 25 foot canoes made of driftwood or pine planks caulked with asphalt. They employed tridents, harpoons and nets woven of sea grass with stone balls to weigh them down. Fishing was best from late spring to late summer when fish schooled and mammals gathered in herds.

The Chumash utilized a similar tactic in hunting seals as did the Plains Indians in hunting buffalo. They would find a herd inland and get between the seals and the open sea, catch them by surprise with sudden screams and then club them to death or spear them as they scampered toward the water.

Those who lived north of San Francisco Bay enjoyed a particularly lucrative environment. The climate was moderate all year and provided an abundance of plants, game and useful raw materials which supported a population of nearly 80,000 Native American Indians.

About 8,000 were Pomo Indians who depended on the White Oaks to provide a steady supply of acorns. The Pomo were good hunters and developed a way to herd deer into a corral where they could be easily killed. They set traps and shot birds from blinds. They also enjoyed nearly 150 miles of fresh water which was loaded with fish and there was an abundance of edible plants, seeds, roots and berries.

They were able to spend time and effort in creating more elaborate homes, using slabs of redwood piled against a center post to create a conical, single family tepee. They lived in areas with about 75-300 individuals but there was no formal structure. Power was left with the males but followed no specific pattern.

Generally the man fished, hunted, built the home and made his tools. The woman gathered edible plants, cooked, tended to the children and wove baskets.

Fishermen of the Northwest

Located along the Northern Pacific Coast, the Indians here focused on fishing. The ocean and rivers were full of fish. Forests grew thick and tall. The large red cedars could be easily split with even crude tools and these Indians built large houses by tying big slabs of cedar to wooden frames. They built canoes for calm waters and made larger vessels as seagoing whaleboats.

They used nets or spears with stone points or bone barbs. The men built weirs and nets especially to catch salmon swimming upstream to spawn. The supply was plentiful and the women smoked a year's supply of the salmon.

While the seed gatherers spent most of their time gathering food, the Indians of the Northwest found an abundant supply, both of fish and meat. The Northwest Indians began to accumulate things and honored wealth. They erected totem poles to call attention to their positions. They painted pictures on their shields and tepees to express their vision.

Whaling was prevalent, but dangerous. They used a large, seagoing dugout canoe made by burning the inside of a tree to hollow it out. Each man was trained to handle his particular responsibility. The leader engaged in elaborate ceremonial activities to enroll the spirits in the hunt. The flesh and skin of the whales were eaten and the intestines used to hold oil. The sinew was used to make strong rope.

Among the Northwest tribes, organization became more important.

Individuals became powerful chieftains with the right to assign hunting and fishing rights. The Haida society had three grades consisting of the aristocrats, the commoners and slaves.

Further north were the Mackenzie-Yukon Caribou Hunters and the Inuit. For them the caribou was the main focus just as the buffalo was for the Plains Indians. They made their tents and clothing of caribou or other deer skins. In winter they tracked game on snowshoes and depended on their dogs to carry their baggage, often pulling it on sleds.

The Inuit Indians continue to live on the frigid northern fringes of the continent. From Alaska to Labrador these hardy survivors depend on seal, whale, walrus, caribou, polar bear and other Artic birds and animals for their survival. They utilize the hides for clothing, turning it inside out to trap the body's heat.

General Characteristics

The Indians didn't spend all of their time in activities just to survive. They engaged in many games and sports. Tribal members gathered for periods as long as a week sometimes. While the main reason for the gathering was usually ceremonial, they spent time in playing games, storytelling and social singing and dancing.

Some games were played for fun, but many were challenging, designed to increase the skill of those participating. The Ball Game was somewhat like lacrosse. It was played with sticks and a ball. The sticks had a looped head with a net. The ball was made from deerskin, stuffed with deer hair. Many tribal members bet on the game using articles of clothing, personal possessions and other items which were held by trusted tribal members until the game was won and the items distributed. It was a rough game. If a player dropped his stick he had to carry the ball with his teeth.

The Native American Indians spoke as many as six hundred dialects which reflected many different languages. This created difficulty in communicating even between tribes only a short distance away from each other. Indians of the Great Plains worked out a sign language with which they could communicate with neighboring tribes.

Structurally the Indians were organized primarily into a village or hunting group which might only include 50 or less people. Neighboring villages which spoke the same language would work together as a unit if the hunting ground provided adequate food.

Children played much as children of today. The girls played with dolls dressed in costumes of their tribes while boys shot small arrows from toy bows and crept through the woods pretending to be hunters or warriors. They played with whip tops, stilts, slings and other toys similar to those of early colonial children. They also had dogs and small wild animals as pets.

Native Americans wore beads and pendants as expressions of their social lives, economic and political concerns and in conformity with their beliefs in cosmology and religion. In the New England area, wampum beads were part of an economy of reciprocity and gift exchange. Reciprocal gifts cemented ties between individuals and nations.

Dance ceremonies celebrated the change of seasons, harvest, births and marriages. They were even used to commemorate more solemn events such as death and were often accompanied by chanting. The term "Powwow" is a word not originally used by the Indians with reference to their dancing ceremonies, but rather adapted from usage by the non-natives and ultimately picked up by the natives. Dancing ceremonies were also a time of joyful gathering and celebration of life. They are more complex than our word "dance" can fully describe.

They encompass both ceremony and prayer which includes all of life, resulting in emotional and spiritual response.

Ceremonies involving healing and curing often required the use of specific kinds of jewelry and ornaments, Shells of many animals such as turtles were utilized in healing ceremonies. Certain necklaces provided protection from particular disorders. Face painting with red colors and red hair ornaments were employed at times in these ceremonies.

When a woman experienced her first menstrual period, she wore a garment which covered her head. Subsequently, she could remove the veil and adorn herself with necklaces, belts and wampum headbands.

Beads were also used in marriage rituals. Bridal presents, including wampum and other trinkets, were given the bride. Funeral ceremonies even featured beads. The deceased often wore necklaces, bracelets, rings, headbands and other ornaments that were provided by relatives.

Woven headwork consisted of beads and string. The string could range from twisted sinew or hide thong, to twisted cord from numerous plants, bark and roots.

Dogbane stalks, basswood bark and cedar bark were also commonly made into a cord for bead weaving.

Native American Indians were accustomed to communal ownership of land. Tribal members used the land within the territorial boundaries of that tribe. No individual owned any of the land and no one, even the tribal chief was authorized to dispose of it. When the colonists bought land from the Indians or their leaders, they bought land that didn't belong to the seller and couldn't be sold according to Indian custom.

In his book, "American Holocaust: Columbus and the Conquest of the New World," David E. Stannard tells of Native Americans living in towns and villages as farmers and describes the majority of Native Societies as being organized democratically, with even the right of women to vote.

The magnificent capital of the Aztec society brought drinking water from natural springs, carrying it into the city by way of an aqueduct system. Over 1000 public workers were assigned to maintain the city's streets and keep them clean.

The Iroquois Confederacy was a union of initially five, now six, independent nations of the Haudenosaunee people. It boasted a democratic government which has been credited with having influenced the Articles of Confederation and the U.S. Constitution. We will have more to say about it later.

Jean Jacques Rousseau wrote that the idea of freedom and democratic ideals was born in America because it was only in this country that Europeans from the period of 1500 to 1776 knew of societies that were truly free.

He wrote, "Natural freedom is the only object of the policy of the Native Americans; with this freedom do nature and climate rule alone amongst the Native Americans . . . . they are people who live without laws, without police, without religion." (Jean Jacques Rousseau, "Jesuit and Savage in New France")

Chapter 2

The Old World Looks Outward

The existence of monarchies and rivaling empires held center stage in the Old World and the search for trading partners and trade goods was prevalent. Most travel was by overland routes and was both slow and difficult. Giovanni de Plano was the first recorded traveler who journeyed to Mongolia and back during the six year span between 1241 and 1247. It was Marco Polo, however, who is most noted for his travels throughout Asia from 1271 to 1295. His explorations were followed and studied by merchants throughout Europe and although most of the trade between Europe and the Middle East was controlled by the Italian city-states, interest in participating in this lucrative trading was spreading to other parts of the European area.

In 1439 Niccolo Da Conti published an account of his visits to India and Southeast Asia which further spread the interest in reaching the lucrative goods to be found in these far off lands. But the obstacles of distance, slow travel and hostile enemies such as the tribesmen of the Ottoman Empire continued to prevent them from getting more actively involved.

Because spices and silk were considered important items of trade, the merchants were anxious to find alternate routes to obtain them. The first great wave of expeditions began in Portugal under Prince Henry the Navigator. His main objective was to explore and chart the West Coast of Africa looking for trade opportunities and potential new land for his kingdom. The Portuguese hoped to be able to circumvent the blockage by the hostile Muslim states of the traditional land routes of North Africa by making voyages on the seas.

The development of the carrack and the caravel designs of ships by the Portuguese made it possible to leave the placid waters of the Mediterranean and Baltic Seas and navigate the more turbulent waters of the open Atlantic Ocean. This opened new possibilities in the search for uncharted ways to reach the desired trade markets of the distant lands of the Far East.

The next two decades found new developments occurring in rapid succession. In 1434 the Papala Bull Romanus Pontifex granted Portugal the trade monopoly for the newly discovered waterways. It was in 1487 that Bartholomeu Dias rounded what is now the Cape of Good Hope, proving that the Indian Ocean was accessible from the Atlantic Ocean. Now the land routes were cut off by the Muslims and Portugal controlled the Indian Ocean access.

Spain, recovering from their victory over the Moorish kingdom of Granada from whom they had been receiving African goods through tribute, began to look westward. There had been a great deal of speculation that a passage to the east could be reached by traveling west in spite of the lingering belief by many that the world was flat and that such a venture might result in falling off the edge.

King Ferdinand II and Queen Isabella decided to fund an exploratory voyage proposed by Christopher Columbus. This devout Christian is quoted as saying, "It was the Lord who put into my mind the fact that it would be possible to sail from here to the Indies. All who heard of my project rejected it with laughter."

He credited the journey to the Indies as the fulfillment of a prophecy in Isaiah rather than the application of intelligence, mathematics or maps.

When they landed on an island in the Bahamas which Columbus called San Salvador they believed that they had landed on outlying islands off India, China, Japan or Indonesia. Columbus noted in his journal that the natives were a gentle and trusting people that could easily be enslaved for the benefit of Spain.

Seeking to locate the Chinese emperor he continued to search the area and ran his flagship, the Santa Maria, aground. Establishing a small fort on the island, he named it Navidad in honor of the Christmas holiday. He left a small number of his crew there and returned to Spain with gold nuggets and jewelry which he presented to Ferdinand and Isabella along with an assurance that he had reached the outskirts of

China or Japan, encouraging them to look forward to a follow up voyage.

His second endeavor in 1493 was more ambitious with 17 ships involved and 1500 persons whose aim was to colonize the area and discover gold and silver. They returned to Navidad only to find the fort in ruins and no evidence of any survivors. A new community was established and the settlers remained there while Columbus continued to explore what he believed to be a part of China. Conditions at Navidad worsened in his absence however, and many chose to return to Spain where the poor conditions in the new world were reported to the Crown.

In 1496 Columbus, himself, left the struggling colony to return to Spain to defend his conduct before the royal officials, leaving his brothers Bartholomew and Diego in charge of the struggling colony. He was not able to take back a great deal of anything valuable to Spain to substantiate his efforts.

He was able, however, to put together another voyage in 1498, but it included only six vessels which were divided into two groups, one to head for the settlement and the other, under the direction of Columbus personally, would continue the search for China. He, too, eventually wound up at Navidad. Conditions were so chaotic that a royal task force was dispatched which arrested Columbus and took him back to Spain in chains where only his past relationship with the king and queen kept him from imprisonment.

Somehow he managed to mount a final effort in 1502 but he was denied entrance to Navidad and so he sailed along the coast of Central America determined to find an opening which would take him to the Far East. Unsuccessful, he had no choice but to make another attempt to visit the colony. He had become ill and his ships were rotting and on the verge of sinking.

His one remaining ship ran aground off of Jamaica and two of his men volunteered to try to reach Navidad by canoe to seek a rescue party for the remaining marooned members. They were successful in reaching their destination but the officials there waited almost a year before going after Columbus and because he knew how unwelcome he was in Navidad, Columbus opted to return directly to Spain.

While the personal desires of Christopher Columbus were noble, he was funded by the King and Queen of Spain who looked for lucrative returns from their investment in his voyage. What's more, his crew members were not on the same page as was he. Enlisting men for such a risky venture did not bring out the elite of society. The trip itself was fraught with danger and controversy. Once on land the crew became even more independent and difficult to control.

He spent most of his remaining years trying to restore his wealth and titles, but in 1504 Isabella died and Ferdinand awarded only partial reinstatement to Columbus which did not include his titles. He died in 1506 unaware that he had discovered a new world.

In 1513, Vasco de Balboa took up the mission and crossed the Isthmus of Panama. He led the first European expedition to see the Pacific Ocean from the west coast of the New World.

Six years later, in 1519, the Spanish crown funded the expedition of a Portuguese navigator named Ferdinand Magellan who completed a voyage around the world. Sailors became certain that the world was indeed round and not flat. He sailed across the Pacific Ocean to the Spice Islands and while killed in a battle in the Philippines, Juan Sebastian Elcano completed the voyage, returning to Portugal three years later.

Other voyages followed and eventually an established route was worked out. The Portuguese were the first westerners to reach Japan and King Manuel I developed a plan to control all the major trade routes of the east through a series of forts and colonies along the way.

It would not be until 1769 that the Bourbon Monarchy of the Spanish empire would expand its presence into the area now known as California and the San Francisco Bay region.

With the opening of the seas to exploration a new era was released. The first English expedition, led by the Italian John Cabot began a series of missions exploring North America. Their motive was still the attempt to find an oceanic route to the northwest that would take them to Asia. While not successful, their discoveries led to the beginning of colonists settling on the east coast of North America.

The exploration of the North American continent began a period of systematic genocide that lasted for over five centuries and is thought to have been the cause of the annihilation of over a hundred million people. Some of the destruction was unplanned in the form of the importation of disease from which the natives lacked natural immunity, but a great deal was the direct result of policies adopted by those in government who practiced expediency and greed regardless of the terrible atrocities that resulted.

Building on the discoveries of Columbus and Balboa, Hernando DeSoto explored North America seeking a northern passage to trade with China. Starting in the year 1539 in what is now Florida he proceeded with a huge army to pass through the areas which today make up Georgia, South and North Carolina and Alabama, then up through Tennessee.

In 1541 he journeyed through Kentucky and Indiana. His scouts reached as far north as Chicago and Lake Michigan, but found no ocean by which to reach China. DeSoto and his men turned southwest and traveled through Illinois, reaching the Mississippi. Disappointed, he continued through Missouri. He became ill in the Ozark Mountains and upon encountering hostile natives, headed toward Mexico City which was Spain's nearest outpost in the New world.

He died, however, in Arkansas and his army continued southward, passing through Louisiana and Texas. Lacking food and water they retreated back to Arkansas where they built boats and drifted down the Mississippi. They were attacked but continued downstream through Louisiana and followed the coast line of Texas, finally reaching Mexico in 1543. Half of them were lost along the way to battle and disease.

Spanish explorers were never again sent deep into the heart of America from the east coast. Instead, they began to develop the areas in Florida and Mexico, abandoning the search for a route to China.

The British colonization of America was one of the most important and their empire in the New World rivaled that of Spain. In 1586 the Roanoke Colony was founded on the Outer Banks of North Carolina but subsequently abandoned. A second attempt the following year (known today as the lost colony) simply disappeared without a trace.

The Jamestown Settlement was founded in 1607 by the London Company in the Colony of Virginia and is considered to be the first permanent English Settlement in the area which subsequently became the United States of America. For 83 years it was the capitol of the Virginia Colony until the village of Williamsburg became the capitol in 1699. Jamestown had been chosen because it provided a defensive position against other European forces which might approach by water and featured a fort. The area was also not inhabited by the local

Indians, primarily because of mosquitoes and a lack of water suitable for drinking.

Starvation, hostile relations with the Indians and a lack of any product for trade threatened its existence, but the introduction of tobacco by colonist John Rolfe saved the day and two years later he married Pocahontas, the daughter of Wahunsonacock, who was the Chief of the Powhatan Confederacy and a period of relative peace with the natives followed.

Activity along the eastern coast was non-stop. In 1607 the Plymouth Company founded the Popham Colony, which was then abandoned the following year. The Plymouth Council for New England founded the Plymouth Colony in 1620 which merged with the Massachusetts Bay Colony in 1691.

It is appropriate to take a special look at the Plymouth experience because we traditionally celebrate Thanksgiving Day as a special day to remember both the blessings of the Lord and the major contribution of the Native American Indians who took mercy on the newcomers in that area and showed them how to grow crops, hunt wild game and live off of the natural resources all around them. The colonists faced danger from disease, hunger, malnutrition, insects and snakes. They lived under unsanitary conditions, had no food for sustenance over the winter months and were not skilled enough to survive on their ability to hunt successfully. Without the assistance of the natives it is doubtful if the Pilgrims could have survived that first year.

We have seen the drive behind the exploration of the New World as the voyagers set forth to find a new route to the lucrative trade with China and to gain wealth and slaves for the ruling powers that financed them. The Pilgrims on the other hand, were driven by something far more substantial. They were seeking freedom to worship their God. Europe consisted of many small countries in which religious policy was dictated by whoever was ruling. Such was the case in England.

They were fleeing the heavy hand of the throne in determining how they would live their lives and follow their conscience in spiritual matters. Gold and valuables, slaves and greater power for the king were not in their play book. So their initial response to the inhabitants was different from that, even of Columbus, who reported that the natives were gentle and would lend themselves nicely to providing slaves for the king.

In 1622 the Province of Maine was begun and later dissolved in 1677. The Province of New Hampshire was settled in 1623 and the Dorchester Company planted an unsuccessful fishing colony on Cape Ann at modern Gloucester, Massachusetts in 1624. Salem Colony settled in what is now known as Salem in Massachusetts in 1628 and it merged with the Massachusetts Bay Colony in the following year when that colony was formed.

The Connecticut Colony was founded in 1633. It merged with Saybrook Colony in 1644 which had been founded in 1635. They were joined by the New Haven Colony, founded in 1638, to become a part of what is now the state of Connecticut. Rhode Island and Providence Plantations were first settled in 1636.

The Province of Maryland was founded in 1634. The Provinces of New York and New Jersey were captured by the English in 1664. Although first settled by Dutch and Swedish immigrants, the Province of Pennsylvania was founded as an English colony in 1681.

Chapter 3

William Penn's Holy Experiment

It is important to look more closely at the influences that caused the different approach by William Penn in Pennsylvania to the Native American Indians who were the inhabitants of the land over which he would have control. It is worth looking beyond his impact on the New World and to consider his motivation and the circumstances which surrounded this unusual man. Darrell Fields provides an excellent account of Penn's contribution in his book "The Seed of a Nation."

Penn's father was a wealthy English aristocrat whose concern for the development of his son was uppermost in his mind. In spite of his father's efforts, however, William developed independently and was greatly influenced by the Quaker religion.

It was on October 31, 1517, that Martin Luther nailed his Ninety-five theses on the door of Castle Church in Wittenberg, Germany, sounding the trumpet for the Reformation to begin throughout the known world.

King Henry of England had problems of his own with the Roman Catholic Church because he wanted to divorce his wife but the Pope refused permission. The king took matters into his own hand and annulled the marriage which caused the Pope to excommunicate him from the church.

This led to an autocracy that consolidated the spiritual and political independence of England. King Henry passed the Act of Supremacy, better known as the Divine Right of Kings, and set up the Church of England. This was the result of the concept that kings were appointed by God and therefore answered to no man.

Future dynasties continued to rule under the Divine Right of Kings and when Queen Elizabeth died in 1603 leaving no heir apparent, the King of Scotland took over and became King James I of England. Under his rule the religious and political structure became so entwined that the monarch became intolerant of those who would not conform to the church and declared them enemies of the state.

A group who wanted to see the church purified from within arose who became known as the Puritans. It was from this group that the Plymouth Colony came into being in Massachusetts. Meanwhile the pot continued to boil in England. King James' son, Charles I, ascended to the throne. He brought both Ireland and Scotland under English control and pushed them to conform to the Church of England.

A rivalry developed between the king and Parliament. The Puritan General Oliver Cromwell sided with Parliament and Charles was defeated. Cromwell rose to the throne, but died in 1658 and was succeeded by Charles II as a result of a rising tide of secularism in England.

It was during these turbulent times that William Penn was born. At the age of twelve God visited William in a very dramatic way. He was at school at the time. His experience was recorded in these words: "He was suddenly surprised with an inward comfort; and as he thought, an external glory filled the room, which gave rise to religious emotions during which he had the strongest conviction of the being of God, and that the soul of man was capable of enjoying communication with Him. He believed also that the seal of Divinity had been put upon him at this moment, or that he had been awakened or called upon to a holy life."

At the age of 16, William Penn entered Christ Church, Oxford. It was here that he was first stirred by the preaching of the Quaker, Thomas Lee. It was here also, that he learned of the desire of the Quakers to have a refuge in the New World.

By May of 1661, Parliament had passed a total of four laws collectively known as the Clarendon Code, which sharply restricted the free exercise of religion, and a year later passed the Quaker Act, making it illegal for Quakers to gather in groups of more than five. Penn was expelled from Oxford for being a non-conformist and too religious.

His father was very upset with his behavior and, determined to separate his son from the Quaker influence. He sent William to Paris for two years. On returning to London from France, he was enrolled in the prestigious law school, Inns of the Court, to study law and rub shoulders with other sons of rich and powerful men. The school closed shortly thereafter because of the plague and Penn was subsequently sent to Ireland to manage the family estate.

Penn had heard the Quaker, Thomas Lee, remark that a person had to "choose between a faith that overcomes the world and a faith that is overcome by the world." He made his decision to select a faith that overcomes the world and became a Quaker.

Religious freedom in England continued to take a downward turn. King Charles looked upon Quakers as rebellious and dangerous. Banishment and sometimes death were the sentences for those who would not stay in line. Penn's very existence often depended upon the favor that his father enjoyed at court. He became a threat to the crown and was imprisoned on six different occasions for preaching the message of Christ from street corners.

In 1670 Penn's father died and he inherited the entire estate. The English government had become a product of countless generations of men ineffectively and brutally attempting to make life work outside of God. In 1680 William Penn petitioned the king for a grant of land in the New World.

Penn's father had loaned the crown large sums of money during England's war with the Dutch. Charles saw an opportunity to get rid of the debt and at the same time get rid of the Quakers. He stipulated, however, that the province be named Pennsylvania in honor of Penn's father.

At the age of thirty-six, William Penn became the proprietor of 28 million acres of land, the largest territory owned entirely by any British citizen in history.

Penn wrote about his new position in 1681, "And because I have been somewhat exercised at time about the nature and end of government among men, it is reasonable to expect that I should endeavor to establish a just and righteous one in this province, that others may take example by it; this truly my heart desires.

"For nations want a precedent, and 'till virtue and sobriety be cherished, the wrath of God will hang over nations. I do, therefore, desire the Lord's wisdom to guide me, and those that may be concerned with me, that we may do the thing that is truly wise and just."

What a pity that Penn's wisdom did not spread and influence others in their approach to dealing with people. He stated very clearly his innermost feelings about Pennsylvania. He believed that God had been instrumental in granting him this wonderful land in the New World and wanted to use that opportunity for the glory of God. He sought to make the operation of his colony to be in accordance with the highest Christian ethic so that it might serve as an example of what man might achieve on earth if he would just put himself in God's hands.

He expected his "Experiment" to be deeply rooted in the Spirit of God and hoped that the province would be filled with virtuous persons who not only knew God's will, but who lived their lives according to His Light so that his "holy experiment" could not fail.

For more than a year, Penn spent time writing and drafting a constitution for Pennsylvania, entitled "The Frame of Government" which was adopted in England on April 25, 1682. He then proceeded to draft an additional set of forty laws which were adopted on May 5, of that same year. One of them required that all men who would hold public office had to have an honest faith in Jesus. He further mandated that freedom of religion would be mandatory.

Penn knew that without the Spirit of God permeating the hearts of men, his ideas would only replace the tyranny of England with the tyranny of fallen humanity, subject not to the king but to the fleshly impulses of many men. Having suffered as he had in England, he knew first-hand the awful advantages governmental powers had when left in the hands of ambitious and self-serving men.

By the time that William Penn received his colony, other colonies had already been established. Jamestown in Virginia, Plymouth in Massachusetts and New Amsterdam, settled by the Dutch all preceded Pennsylvania. Many European colonies claimed to have been founded in the name of religious freedom but that concept was in its infancy and the "right to rule" remained dominant. Native American Indians were given no part in the new world.

Penn's approach to the Indians would prove to be different. He was determined to love them and show them genuine respect. He would treat them the same as the colonists, establishing a framework that included and embraced Native Americans.

When Penn arrived on the shores of the Delaware River he encountered the Lenape Indians who included three different clans belonging to the Algonquian linguistic family. They greeted and welcomed him and negotiations began almost immediately about the acquisition of land along the river where he would soon lay out the city of Philadelphia.

Even though Penn had been given the land by the king, he recognized that the real owners were the inhabitants. Even so, the Natives did not believe that land, something that had been given them by their Creator, could be sold. Between 1682 and 1684 he instituted ten treaties with them through which he secured, with their willing consent, the greater part of southeastern Pennsylvania. They were treaties of covenant for the cohabitation of two nations.

During the first years of Pennsylvania history, when the government was administered according to Christian principles of doing justice and applying patience and forbearance, there were no garrisons, forts, soldiers or muskets within all of its boundaries. None were needed. The Natives intermingled with the colonists, without carrying bows and arrows or tomahawks. All weapons were put aside with the complete assurance that neither would harm the other.

Without war, conquests, revolutions, or struggle, Penn had accomplished a model settlement. He treated the Natives humanely and rationally, as fellow creatures. He walked with them, joined them in their sports, learned their language and sympathized with their troubles. He sought always to be completely fair with them. Among the Indians, Penn became known as the "white truth teller."

In June of 1683 Penn and the Delaware met at Shakamaxon, the capitol city of the Delaware Nation (today a part of the city of Philadelphia), for what has become known as the most historically celebrated treaty between North American Indians and white men. It was not to buy or sell land, but to celebrate and confirm a friendship of love and commitment.

In 1684, after just two years in his province, Penn was forced to return to England to settle border disputes arising between Lord Baltimore of Maryland and Pennsylvania. Confusion existed as to the running of the true fortieth degree latitude marking the boundary between the two colonies. Settlement of the dispute would not occur until after Penn had died and much blood had been shed on the part of the colonists. It is the present Mason Dixon Line.

Shortly after Penn's departure, the people of Pennsylvania began to focus on themselves and to forget to nurture the Godly seed that had been planted. The very things that Penn had warned against were pursued and as an absentee governor, he could exercise little control over the colonists.

In the meantime, France, like England, was contending for a claim in the New World. The French explorer Samuel de Champlain founded a colony of New France in a land called "Cannata."

They began to push along the St. Lawrence River which connects the Great Lakes and the interior of America to the Atlantic Ocean. They established the settlements of Quebec in 1508 and Montreal in 1611.

Because of their nearness to the northern boundaries of the American colonies, England feared a possible invasion of New York and Pennsylvania. Penn also recognized the potential danger and recommended the formation of a continental congress in order to combine the strengths of each of the colonies but his suggestion was ignored.

It was 1699 before Penn was able to physically return to Pennsylvania. His home at Pennsbury Manor had been completed but he was disappointed with the condition of the colony and made a fourth revision to the Constitution which was adopted in 1701 (the Charter of Privileges) and remained the state Constitution until 1776.

In November of that year he was forced to return once again to England because the crown was considering suspending all colonial proprietary governments, including Pennsylvania. Protecting the rights of his colony demanded his presence back in England. He died in 1718 at Ruscombe, in Buckinghamshire, England at the age of seventy-four.

During his lifetime there was no serious trouble between his colony and the Indians, but less than a generation after his death the Delaware, who had welcomed him with open arms, joined the Shawnee in revolt following a long series of injustices perpetrated by the English. The Indians spread terror and destruction throughout the Pennsylvania settlement.

Their treaty of love and friendship lasted for 73 years, but Penn's Holy Experiment was rapidly becoming just a memory because of outside influences and an abandonment of the principles upon which it had been founded.

In 1751, to celebrate the fiftieth anniversary of Penn's "Charter of Privileges," a bell was forged in England. To properly commemorate the purpose, the bell was inscribed with words from Leviticus 25; 10 which read, "Proclaim liberty throughout the land unto all the inhabitants thereof." The bell was hung in the state house in Philadelphia.

It was this same bell which was rung in 1776 when the Declaration of Independence was read in Philadelphia and is now remembered for its ringing on that occasion, although originally created to honor William Penn and his "Charter of Privileges." It just happened to be handy for the occasion in 1776. Still, it was the principles found in Penn's Carter of Privileges which became the foundation of the Articles of Confederation and the Constitution of the United States.

The overriding objective of the colonists up and down the coast was survival. Except for William Penn, the other settlers assumed an attitude of ownership as a result of their discovery of this new land.

Little, if any thought was given to the natural reaction of those who had lived on the land for generations nor to the realization that these newcomers were not only moving in, but insisting that they, the original inhabitants, had to move out.

Two very different motivations existed, both of which were very strong and understandable, but because of their opposition to each other, were destined to create constant hostility. As the newcomers increased in number and permanence, the volatility increased. It is again necessary for us in this day of instant communication to realize that news spread at a very slow pace without telephone, radio, TV or the internet. It traveled at an even slower pace throughout the disconnected Indian nations.

While it is true that there existed mutual savagery, the fact of the matter is that the colonists were intruders who had superior weapons and knowledge in warfare as well as strength in numbers which was utilized in a directed effort against disorganized and sporadic forces. The original welcoming attitude of the natives changed as the motivation and selfishness of the invaders became more evident.

It is also important to note that the relationship of the Cherokee Indians with the newcomers was another example of how peaceful coexistence might have been the outcome of the development of the new nation. This is examined more fully in connection with the "Trail of Tears" in Chapter 6, "Some of the Atrocities the Indians Suffered."

Chapter 4

The Spread of Civilization

Life in the New World was not easy. Our history books have documented the challenges that faced the newcomers up and down the coast. The English were always fearful of an attack from the Spanish to their south and the French to their north. As the colonists faced the many difficulties that they encountered each day they became more and more independent. While the British throne continued to be in charge, there was little that the king did to make their lives any easier and it was a natural reaction that they resented the interference that came with taxes and artificially imposed regulation.

They had to build their own shelters, raise their own food, make their own clothing and care for their sick. Most of their leaders were entrenched in the concept of the right of the king to rule, but in the wilderness where nature was harsh and danger a constant threat, they saw little reason to be loyal to an absentee ruler. Life was indeed difficult and solutions were home grown. Loyalty to God was a strong influence and indeed it helped, not only to keep order, but to motivate one family to help another. While individual effort was the key to success, neighborly assistance often was the deciding factor between success and failure.

It was the Circuit Riders who traveled from one location to another, taking the Good News of eternal life and expounding the message of the need for individual responsibility and righteousness that created an atmosphere that enabled the thirteen colonies to unite in a truly unique fashion. There would be a surrender of individual freedom to form a government that was to provide certain necessities to facilitate community while reserving to each the guarantee of the right to worship according to one's conscience and to freely pursue happiness and personal security.

Before that could happen there was a need to cut off the ties with the king.

The Revolutionary War was long and costly but it bound together even more closely the colonists who now assumed an identity of their own. A new nation was born with new responsibilities and new possibilities. However, the need or desire to include the Native Americans in this new creation died with the death of William Penn. Indeed, they remained a persistent thorn in the side of expansion and exploration. "One Nation, Under God," did not extend to those who originally inhabited the land.

Trouble began early. Although the Indians met the newcomers originally with curiosity and friendship, it was a friendship rarely returned. Spanish conquistadores plundered the Indian villages and enslaved and murdered the inhabitants. The Spanish colonists who followed forced Indians to work in mines and on large estates to produce goods to send back to Spain.

In New England where the Indians helped the settlers build their settlements and taught them how to raise crops and hunt, they were repaid with violence in many instances. One of the earliest bloody battles between Indians and the white newcomers occurred in Connecticut when the colonists attacked the principle village of the Pequot Indians and killed about 600 of the natives, literally destroying the entire tribe. Various tribes formed an alliance to resist such attacks.

The situation became even more complicated as the French and the English went to war for dominance in the New World and enlisted Indians as allies. Some helped the French, others helped the English. In 1763, Pontiac, an Ottawa chief and ally of the French led attacks on English positions in the area of the Great Lakes. The war ended in that same year and when the French made peace with the English, Pontiac also made peace.

The British secured aid from the Indians in the Revolutionary War, but it was of little value to the English forces. It did, however, promote retaliation by Continental Army forces which then proceeded to attack Iroquois Indians located in New York.

Following the Revolution, the United States hoped to maintain peace with the Indians on the frontier. George Washington and several of the founding fathers of the United States thought that the Native American Indians could be made civilized according to European standards. This was the core thinking of dealing with these inconvenient dwellers who resented that their homes were being taken over by invaders. How uncivilized a reaction on their part as to want to prevent that?

Between the years of 1789 and 1812, thirty-four statutes were passed dealing with Native American Indians. The situation became more acute as the settlers moved about and their settlements expanded. The frontier moved consistently westward in search of land, minerals and gold and in each case the "pesky" Indians were in the way.

In 1789 Congress passed an act providing $20,000 for the expenses "which may attend negotiations or treaties with the Indian Tribes" and provided for commissioners to manage the same. It increased the amount of money by another $20,000 during the following year and in a subsequent law that same year, made it illegal "for anyone other than with government permission to trade with, or make a treaty with any Indian nation."

The government recognized a need to regulate agreements made with the Indians through a single regulatory body which logically was the federal government. In 1793 a section of the law to regulate trade and treaties with the Indians granted the president the authority to provide assistance to promote civilization among the friendly Indian tribes.

In 1793 a sum of $100,000 was appropriated for negotiating with the hostile Indian tribes northwest of the Ohio River. In 1795, $50,000 was appropriated for the purchase of goods from Indians within the United States, the sale of which would be under the direction of the president. In 1796 Congress granted permission for the president to establish trading houses for the purpose of conducting trade with the Indians for a period of two years.

On May 6, 1796, money was appropriated to cover the costs of a treaty signed at Greenville on August 3, 1795 with the Wyandot, Delaware, Shawnee, Ottawa, Chippewa, Potawatomi, Miami, Eel River, Weea, Kickapoo, Piankashaw, and Kaskaskia Indians. It established specific amounts of an annuity to be paid annually according to the stipulations of the treaty.

On May 19 of that same year a boundary line was drawn between the United States and various Indian tribes which started at the mouth of the Cayahoga River on Lake Erie in the north and wound its way south to modern day South Carolina. It was a complicated, but specific, designation of land that was established for the displaced Native Americans by Congress.

Indeed, the land appropriated was such that if all reservations were located in areas that offered the potential that this land offered, perhaps the situation which exists today could have been avoided. Even more importantly, if the United States had lived up to its promises, and honored its agreements things would have gone far more peacefully. Over three hundred fifty treaties were signed and every one was broken.

From the white man's point of view the problem of communal ownership of land and religious prohibitions of selling it was a major obstacle. Consensual decision-making was another and a lack of a central authority with power to make binding deals muddied the water even further. They were slow, they were democratic and they would not agree to give up their land, so they had to go.

Military force, treaties, manipulation through deceit and more recently the courts have been used to accomplish the goal of disruption of Indian sovereignty and autonomy.

As the settlers migrated west they settled on Indian lands and they demanded and received protection from the Army. Tecumseh, a Shawnee chief, organized several tribes to prevent the loss of any more Indian lands, but he was defeated at Tippecanoe in 1811 by General William Henry Harrison.

Many Indians supported the British in the War of 1812. Once the war ended and the United States was once again secure in its boundaries, federal policy turned to the removal of Indians east of the Mississippi to the land known as the great American Desert. To implement this policy, Congress passed The Indian Removal Act which was signed by President Andrew Jackson on May 28, 1830 giving him the authority to exchange land west of the Mississippi for the southeastern territory of the Five Civilized Tribes (Cherokee, Creek, Choctaw, Chickasaw and Seminole). This policy caused Jackson to clash with the Supreme Court who had earlier ruled in favor of the right of the Cherokee Indians to retain their lands in Georgia. Jackson refused to recognize the court's ruling and the Cherokee were forced to leave and head westward to Indian Territory in several stages which has become known as the "Trail of Tears," more fully described in Chapter 6.

The story really begins with the Choctaw nation which was living in the area presently comprising the states of Alabama, Mississippi and Louisiana. A series of treaties reduced the land on which these people were able to live to 11,000,000 acres. The treaty of Dancing Rabbit Creek gave the remaining land to the United States in 1831 and was only signed after a number of the Choctaw were allowed to remain.

Under the direction of George Gaines, appointed by Secretary of War, Lewis Cass, the process was spread out over three phases. The first was met with flash floods, sleet and snow. Original plans called for the Indians to be transported by wagon, but flooding waters cancelled those plans.

Five steamboats were obtained. From Memphis a group traveled up the Arkansas River for about 60 miles to Arkansas Post. Freezing temperatures made further travel by water impossible and with food supplies running out, forty government wagons were commandeered to transport them to Little Rock. Food rationing consisted of a handful of boiled corn, one turnip and two cups of heated water each day. Upon reaching Little Rock, the Choctaw chief was quoted as describing the trip as a "trail of tears and death."

A second group, departing from Vicksburg, was led by an incompetent guide and was lost in the Lake providence swamps. In all, about 17,000 Choctaw Indians made the move to the territory now known as Oklahoma. It is estimated that between 2,500 and 6,000 died along the way.

Those who chose to remain in Mississippi were treated badly. They were harassed and intimated, reporting having homes torn down and burned, fences destroyed, cattle turned loose and individuals scourged, manacled, fettered and personally abused causing many to die. This treatment was at the hands of the civilized white settlers.

In 1832 the Seminole Indians living in Florida were called to a meeting at Payne's Landing on the Oklawaha River. Florida had been acquired from Spain in 1821. The Indians were informed that a treaty had been negotiated calling for them to move west where they would rejoin the Creek nation from which they had separated themselves many years earlier. A delegation of seven chiefs would inspect the land where they were to go and determine if it was suitable. The delegation was gone for several months and reportedly signed a statement saying that the land was indeed suitable, but upon returning to Florida, some denied having signed at all, while others said that they had been forced to sign.

At any rate, these chiefs were not empowered to decide the fate of all the tribes involved. Those residing in the area of the Apalachicola River decided to go. They left in 1834. A year later, a group of Seminole Indians ambushed a U.S. Army company which was attempting to forcibly remove some of the Indians, killing 110 of the soldiers and starting a major conflict.

The St. Augustine Militia requested guns from the U.S War Department and 500 volunteers were mobilized under Brigadier General Richard K. Call. Seminole war parties raided farms and settlements. The residents went to nearby forts, into town or to other communities entirely.

One war party, led by Osceola attacked a Florida militia supply train. Eight guards were killed and six others wounded. Sugar plantations along the Atlantic coast south of Augustine were destroyed and many slaves joined the Indians. Fighting lasted for nearly ten years at a cost of nearly $20,000,000. Captured Seminoles were forcibly removed to the west. Some escaped into the Everglades.

The situation in Georgia was a series of incidents of subterfuge and mistrust.

Following the War of 1812 some Muscogee leaders signed treaties that turned over more Indian land to Georgia. Two years later the Treaty of Fort Jackson was signed which essentially ended resistance by the Creek nation.

Andrew Jackson chastened the friendly Indians for not cutting Tecumseh's throat when they had a chance and said the entire Creek nation had to pay expenses which he calculated to be 23,000,000 acres of land. It did not matter that they had helped achieve victory. The treaty of Indian Springs was signed which relinquished most of whatever land remained in Creek control in the state of Georgia.

Subsequently the Creek National Council succeeded in getting that Treaty nullified because it was fraudulent. President John Quincy Adams agreed and signed the Treaty of Washington but Governor Troup ignored the new treaty and renewed forcible removal of the remaining Creeks. President Adams at first attempted to intervene with federal troops but then acquiesced, not wanting to get involved in a civil war. "The Indians are not worth going to war over'" he said.

About 20,000 Creeks from other tribes remained in Alabama. The state moved to abolish tribal governments and impose state laws over the Creeks. An appeal to Andrew Jackson fell on deaf ears and the treaty of Cusseta was signed which divided up the land into individual lots allowing those who chose to sell their land to the state and go west to do so, while those who chose to remain could stay but were subject to Alabama state law.

Once again civilized whites moved in as land speculators and squatters began to defraud Creeks out of their allotments causing violence and the Creek war to begin. Secretary of War Lewis Cass sent General Winfield Scott to end the violence and forcibly remove the Creeks to Indian Territory west of the Mississippi. For a land of law, it appeared to be administered according to skin color.

Chapter 5

The Indian Wars

From 1540 through 1890 there was a continued period of conflict between the invading white settlers and the Native American Indians. What the Indians had, the white man wanted, including his land for farming, his fields for grazing of cattle, his forests for hunting and his minerals for mines. And they were determined to get them by whatever means were necessary. To the white man the Indians were savages who were unable to wisely utilize their possessions, completely ignoring the fact that these people had survived successfully on this land for thousands of years.

Despite early attempts by the natives to deal honestly with the intruders, dishonesty and deceit championed the response of the ever-increasing flow of immigrants from Europe to the once quiet lands of the natives. To the Indians, the white man and his army became a constant source of fear and aggravation. But, because of their culture, they saw the intrusion of the army as just another tribe. They could not comprehend the long term threat that the white man posed.

We have attempted to show the fervor with which the "civilized" European adventurers sought to add land and treasure to the royal coffers of their homeland, whether it was England, France, Spain or the newly formed nation seeking to colonize the New World. For all of them the unanswerable question remained. "What to do with the people who already lived here and called it their home?"

We have also suggested that William Penn in his "Holy Experiment" offered a solution which worked well during his lifetime and under his leadership, resulted in peaceful cohabitation with the original inhabitants of Penn's Woods. Unfortunately it went the way of all greedy and dishonest wielders of power once Penn was gone.

The era under consideration is rampant with broken treaties and promises by the United States government to the natives who presented an ongoing challenge. For more than three and a half centuries the problem of what to do with the Indians arose repeatedly. It was part of the growing pains of a civilization with no understanding of the full potential of its own expansion. The West was for the most part an unknown quantity.

Clearly the policy of the U.S. government was, "We are right and these inconvenient people will have to become like us to survive." In spite of the undeniable language of the Declaration of Independence regarding the equality of mankind, it became interpreted early on to mean the equality of those who signed it and did not include the original inhabitants of the land. Nor did it include the people captured in Africa and forcibly removed from their homeland to be sold as slaves to the highest bidder in this country.

The right to own property clearly referred to those citizens by whom and for whom this document had been created. Obviously, it had no reference to the people who had lived on this land called America for centuries and who no longer had any right to their homes.

Search and seizure without cause also had no meaning where the Indians were concerned. In fact, in spite of their longstanding habitation of this land, since the natives had no papers from the European royalty, they therefore had no legal standing to remain in their homes and they were routinely uprooted.

At first, they were helpful to the newcomers. As noted earlier, we celebrate Thanksgiving because of the bounty of God, but also with a clear understanding that had it not been for the help of the Indians, the Pilgrims would not likely have survived that first harsh winter.

The Jamestown settlers believed that the Indians would welcome them and willingly supply food in exchange for European tools and Christianity. They did not realize that the Indians lived very close to the subsistence level by hunting regularly for food and gathering little more than enough to meet their immediate needs, so that it would be available when the need subsequently arose. To the Native, it was acceptable for someone else in need to come along later and take what was needed.

The settlers, however, wiped out the supply and left none for anyone else, putting the sustenance of the natives at risk.

Relationships deteriorated further when the settlers allowed their cattle to wander onto Indian cornfields. When the white man used his superior firepower to force the Indians to contribute food, Chief Powhatan began to express displeasure. Relations were improved temporarily when John Wolfe married Pocahontas, his daughter.

But, following her death and the subsequent death of her father, a new chief, Opechancanough, took control of the confederacy formerly led by Powhatan. He acted as though he had an interest in Christianity and invited settlers to move further inland onto native lands. Then, in March of 1622, he led a surprise attack on the scattered white settlements, killing nearly 350 whites. Livestock were slaughtered as well and crops were burned.

The uprising caused the Virginia Company to declare bankruptcy. In 1624 Virginia was made a royal colony and would remain so until independence was won.

Warfare continued for another ten years with no decisive battle being won by either side, but the settlers gave up on any pretense of coexisting with the natives and a policy of extermination ensued. Extensive land concessions were made by the Indians in 1632 in the western Chesapeake Bay area.

In 1644 another effort to resist was mounted by the natives and more than 400 settlers were killed. In 1646 Opechancanough, who lived to be a 100 years old, was captured and died.

In the meantime, the Pequot tribe, which was located along the Thames River in present day Connecticut, was the focus of trouble as the colonists began expanding westward. Unfair trading, alcohol, destruction of Pequot crops by cattle belonging to the colonists and the ongoing intrusion on tribal hunting ground became the focal points of friction between the two groups.

In July 1636, John Oldham, a white man, was killed by the Indians. Although he was of questionable character, the incident prompted the Governor, John Endicott to call out the militia. Forming an alliance with the Mohegan and Narragansett tribes, the colonists attacked a Pequot village on the Mystic River in May of 1637.

They set fire to the Indian dwellings and then shot the inhabitants as they fled their burning homes. Somewhere between 400 and 700 native men, women and children were killed and many of those who managed to survive being shot were sold into slavery in Bermuda.

Chief Sassacus of the Pequot tribe was captured by the Mohawks and executed. The devastation of the homes and lives of men, women and children set an unfortunate precedent for future actions in battles between the colonists and the Indians.

The lands east of the Narragansett Bay, which stretched to Cape Cod, were occupied by the Wampanoag tribe headed by Chief Massasoit who was the major player in the support given to the Pilgrims in their early days. Massasoit had created a harmonious relationship with the colonists, but as time passed and the colonists expanded their boundaries, tribal lands diminished and tensions increased.

In 1662, Metacom, a son of Massosoit, became chief. He was known to the colonists as King Philip. Accelerated Indian dependence on English manufactured goods led to increased land sales and decreased Indian land. In 1675, three tribal members were tried and executed by the English for the murder of a converted Wampanoag Indian which resulted in a year of hostilities.

The Wampanoag tribe, equipped with armor and rifles, attacked a number of settlements, killing dozens of men, women and children. The English responded by destroying native villages and killing the inhabitants. This led to the entrance of other tribes into the fray which created havoc in the entire area.

In 1676 the Narragansett tribe, which had joined the uprising, was soundly defeated and their chief killed. Shortly thereafter, King Philip was betrayed, captured and executed. His head was put on a stake and paraded throughout the Plymouth Colony. His son was captured and sold into slavery in Bermuda. Other captives were made to serve in homes throughout New England.

It would take more than twenty years before the devastation to the colonial properties could be repaired. The natives in New England were so badly defeated that resistance by them to the advance of the colonists became almost non-existent. Nonetheless, further expansion by the colonists was delayed for many more years.

While the English colonists were experiencing difficulty in their relation with the natives, the Spanish regularly inflicted cruelty and barbarism on the natives who were denied the right to practice their native religion under penalty of death.

Torture was even utilized in efforts to cause the natives to convert to Christianity.

In New Mexico, the Spaniards took a portion of every Indian farmer's crops to support their missionary, military and civil institutions. Forced Indian labor was used to farm the fields and to work as weavers in manufacturing shops. Finally the Inquisition, which was an all-out holy war on anything which was not Franciscan Christian, allowed the Spaniards to declare Native Indians heretics and witches and condemn them to years of slavery.

This inhumane treatment of the natives finally led to the Pueblo Revolt of 1680 which overcame the Spanish rule and allowed the Indians to live independently for a period until the Spanish returned a dozen years later.

During the period between 1740 and 1748 the French began building forts in the country west of the Allegheny Mountains in what is today the state of Ohio. Essentially they wanted to maintain control of the lucrative fur-trapping and trading and keep out the advancing American colonists.

At the same time the British crown had given a huge land grant to a group of Virginians which led to the creation of the Ohio Company. It was created specifically to invest in western lands and beef up British fur trading activities.

In 1753, George Washington and a small group of Virginians were sent to ask the French to leave the area. The French refused to go. Washington was attracted to a spot where the Ohio River begins (now the location of the city of Pittsburgh). On his recommendation British officials dispatched a construction detail to establish a fort, but the French got wind of the plan and sent a much larger force of soldiers who drove the British detail away and proceeded to complete the structure themselves, naming it Fort Duquesne.

Gov. Robert Dinwiddie once more looked to George Washington. At the age of 22, he led a force against the French who were reinforced with Indian forces who considered the French less of a threat than the British.

Washington was successful and he quickly ordered the construction of a fort which was called Fort Necessity in the area known as the Great Meadows, not far from the original site of Fort Duquesne. The French counter-attacked and after a one day battle, Washington surrendered and returned to Virginia. However, the first of many skirmishes between the two countries had begun and the conflict, which became known as the French and Indian War, continued for the next seven years.

The war was actually fought in three stages. The first phase focused on the colonial holdings in North America and consisted largely of attempts by each nation to capture the opponent's forts established along the new frontier.

In its second stage the war carried over into Europe and new alliances influenced the battles. However, no decision was reached and the concentration returned once again to North America where the increased investment of large amounts of money and new military talent won the day for the British.

In the meantime, unrest with the natives in the New World continued. In 1710, a settlement established by some German and Swiss settlers was begun along the Neuse River in the area of northern North Carolina. Once again encroachment and unfair trading practices incited the natives to war. The Tuscarora Indians, under Chief Hancock, attacked the village of New Bern along with other settlements in the area. Hundreds of the white settlers were killed and their homes and crops were destroyed.

The Tuscarora Indians remained in control until 1713 when Captain James Moore, reinforced by Yamasee Indians, defeated them at their village of Neoheroka. A number of the captured Tuscarora were sold into slavery to help pay the costs of the battle. The remaining natives were forced to leave the area. They wound up in New York, later becoming a part of the Iroquois Confederation.

Further south the Yamasee Indians, who originally inhabited the area now making up northern Florida and southern Georgia, had been forced to leave their homelands and they migrated into what later became South Carolina. At first they got along with the British settlers there, but once again the increasing number of white settlers put a severe strain on the Indian agriculture and hunting lands.

As conditions worsened, in the spring of 1715, the Yamasee formed an alliance with several other tribes and attacked the white settlements, killing several hundred white settlers and destroying both homes and crops. The frontier was abandoned with the surviving settlers fleeing to North Carolina, some even as far north as Virginia seeking safety.

An ultimate reprisal against the Yamasee found them outnumbered and they were pushed back to their original territory in northern

Florida. Here they engaged in warfare with the Creeks who just about eliminated them except for a few who joined forces with the Seminole Indians.

The fighting had long lasting consequences in the area. It took almost ten years before the settlers were willing to re-enter the area and when they did the prior destruction of their livestock caused them to shift their attention from farming to the utilization of trees which produced tar, pitch and turpentine in addition to the lumber itself. Naval stores, rice and indigo became mainstays of the economy.

In the northwest, Ottawa Chief Pontiac wanted to restore the lost lands in the Detroit area to his people and he developed a plan to bring together all the tribes within an area of 200,000 square miles to form an army to defeat the British settlers. He held a grand council in 1763 attended by 60 other chiefs, formulating a plan to simultaneously attach Fort Detroit and the forts at Green Bay, Mackinac, Sandusky and St. Joseph.

Pontiac led the attack on Fort Detroit personally. On May 8, 1783, he and his team gained entrance to the Council House. He was to present a wampum belt to the commandant, Major Gladwin. His men wore blankets draped over their shoulders to conceal sawed-off shotguns.

It had been pre-arranged that the awarding of the belt would provide the signal for the attack. The Major had been forewarned, however, and before the Indian chief made his presentation, his soldiers surrounded the invaders and disarmed them.

Pontiac made another effort to gain entrance a few days later, but was unsuccessful. Angry, he began a prolonged attack on the British which lasted 153 days. The Commandant closed the fort and dispatched patrols with orders to burn houses and any buildings which blocked the view of the defenders in the fort. Pontiac carefully watched for any activity which might attempt to provide supplies to the victims of the siege. He scalped and mutilated all who were captured and put them on display to create fear in the minds of the defending soldiers.

On the 29th of July, a convoy with supplies under the command of Captain Dalzell made it safely up the river to the fort. The newly arrived officer and a force of 250 set out to attack the Indians. The route to the Indian camp was full of lookouts and Pontiac was warned well in advance of the attack and he set up an ambush which killed Captain Dalzell and a large number of his men. Only about ninety men survived and no further attempts to defeat the Indians were made from the fort.

Supplies did arrive by way of two ships in spite of efforts by Pontiac to disrupt their arrival. Pontiac, however, continued his siege until word arrived in 1763 that peace had been declared between the French and British forces which meant that the French would no longer assist the Indians in their efforts. With the loss of French support and the return of many of his allies to their own territories, Pontiac sought peace with Major Gladwin. He and his warriors returned to their native land along the Maumee River.

Ironically, Detroit was the only fort in the original plan that was not destroyed. All the others were captured and destroyed. Pontiac signed a peace treaty in 1767 and two years later was killed by a blow from a hatchet from a Kaskaskian Indian.

The Peace of Paris, which ended the Seven Years' War between France and England and its counterpart in North America, included a pledge by the British to abandon further expansion west of the Appalachian Mountains.

Five years later the Iroquois Confederacy signed a treaty with the British, surrendering any claim to lands south and east of the Ohio River. However, white settlers crossed the Appalachians and some continued on beyond the Ohio River. Clashes between the two races became common place.

The Governor of Virginia was John Murray. He prepared a two pronged offensive. The first was an assault on the natives in the area now known as West Virginia and a second, which he led personally, headed toward Fort Pitt in Pennsylvania.

The defining battle took place in the Little Kanawha Valley. The presence of British soldiers on native lands convinced the chief of the Shawnee Indians to alter earlier plans of moderation and to join in the action. He formed a large war party but in the Battle of Point Pleasant on October 10, 1774, he and his braves were defeated and pushed northward to villages on the other side of the Ohio.

The Shawnee, Mingo and Delaware later signed the Treaty of Camp Charlotte in which they agreed to allow free navigation on the Ohio River, return all captives and release their claims to the lands south and east of the Ohio River, joining the Iroquois who had earlier signed a similar treaty.

The pattern kept repeating itself in one area of the new nation after another. Efforts at getting along peacefully apparently worked for short periods of time, but with the passage of time, the white invaders continued to expand and the existence of natives was an unavoidable reality with which they had to deal.

As the New Nation began to coalesce, it attempted to deal with problems of growth and concerns from within and without. Congressional leaders were concerned foremost for the safety of the settlers on the frontier.

Following the signing of the Treaty of Greenville in 1795 relative peace prevailed between the white settlers and the natives of the Old Northwest. The administrations of George Washington and John Adams had attempted to abide by the terms of the treaties between the government and the natives, but Thomas Jefferson was anxious to obtain more agricultural land for the settlers and entered into a series of land purchases through treaties.

Tecumseh, a Shawnee chieftain, and his brother Tenskwatawa, better known as the Prophet, resented the constant upheaval of his people. He attempted to end the further sale of land to the whites as well as to resist alcohol and other vices of the two competing cultures. A new native village was built in Indiana where the rivers of Wabash and Tippecanoe came together. It became the center of Tecumseh's efforts to bring together the tribes east of the Mississippi, hoping to stop the spread of the white invasion.

In 1811 William Henry Harrison, governor of the Indiana Territory and superintendent of the Northwest Indians, headed a military strike force. With an army of 1,100 men he marched toward the new village, known as Prophet's town.

Shortly before dawn they attacked. After a fierce two hour battle the natives were forced to flee. Tecumseh was away on a recruiting mission.

The victory greatly improved the safety of the settlements in the territory. The confederation which had been formed was disintegrated and Tecumseh stayed away for almost three months before returning and, although remaining a thorn in the side of the Americans, he later joined with them in the War of 1812.

An extract from Dr. Andrew P. Hay, surgeon to the army under the command of Governor Harrison dated: Fort Harrison, 70 miles above Vincennes on the Wabash, Nov. 10, 1811: "The troops marched from this place, twelve days ago, towards the Shawanoe prophet's town. I was ordered unwillingly to take charge of all the sick of the army who were left here.

"An express has just arrived from the army. The troops reached the neighborhood of the town on last Thursday, and marched up within gun shot. Some of the chiefs came out to see the governor, to know his intentions; they told him if he was for fighting, they would fight. The governor told them he wanted peace. They then agreed to have a consultation next day and told the governor that he need not be afraid of anything that night. The governor marched a mile from town, and formed his camp, expecting all would be well. But about two hours before day the treacherous Indians attacked the camp—the centinels discovered them—fired and the alarm was raised. Some of the Indians rushed forward with tomahawks and were in the camp before the lines were formed—a general engagement took place, and the Indians were completely routed before day light. I am told the regulars behaved well during the engagement; pin'd the savages to the ground with their bayonets, whilst they were using their tomahawks—a fearful sight to those who never saw infighting.

"There were betwixt twenty to thirty of our troops left dead on the ground, a great number wounded, many dangerously—about sixty Indians were found dead.—But we have to regret the loss of many brave and valuable citizens. They died gloriously.

"The army is now on the return—the surgeons have their hands full. I regret that I'm not with the wounded. They will be here in a few days."

Within the Native American population there was a great deal of pressure to go along with the white man's program of civilization. Benjamin Hawkins, a federal agent to the Creek Indians had put in place a program that featured the planting of cotton and other cash crops, the purchase of private property and even the owning of African slaves.

To many of the natives, this idea appealed because it offered a way to live in peace. To more traditional natives, the giving up of sacred ceremonies and traditions was unacceptable. A visit from the Shawnee chief Tecumseh resulted in strong opposition among the Upper Creek of central Alabama. He preached a strong reliance on traditional ways and opposition to the white man's invasion of land owned by their forefathers.

These Upper Creek were known as the Red Sticks and considered hostile by the white settlers. The Lower Creek were known as the White Sticks who aligned themselves with the settlers. On August 30, 1813 the Red Stick set upon an American stockade on the Alabama River called Fort Mims and killed more than 350 Americans and Indians.

This resulted in the entrance of the armed forces and a counter attack was assembled by forces from Tennessee, Mississippi and Georgia with the lead being taken by General Andrew Jackson of Tennessee.

They attacked the Indian village of Talishatchee and another Creek stronghold at Talladega. Meanwhile a force from Georgia under General John Floyd attacked the village of Auttosee on the Tallapoosa River, killing two hundred Red Creeks. Mississippi volunteer forces burned the village of the Red Stick leader, William Weatherford, also known as Red Eagle. Both Cherokee and White Creek Indians participated in all three of these battles on the side of the federal forces.

On March 27, 1814, General Andrew Jackson's forces killed between 850 and 900 Red Stick Indians at the Horseshoe Bend of the Tallapoosa River, capturing over 500 women and children. This defeat broke the power of the Red Stick and many fled to Florida to join the Seminoles, while others simply went into hiding.

Typical of the inconsistency of the official policy, the White Sticks, who were allies in the civil battles against the Red Sticks, were also forced to sign the treaty of Fort Jackson on August 9, 1814 and give up more than 20 million acres of land in the areas which now form Georgia and Alabama.

Adding insult to injury, these increased lands led to greater expansion by the settlers which subsequently forced the Creeks to be removed westward to Indian Territory in 1835 and 1836.

The Seminole Indians occupied territory essentially permitted by the Spanish in order to maintain a buffer between their colonies and the British. However, these lands were quite desirable and so became the object of much interest to American settlers. In addition, the Seminoles had become a safe haven for runaway slaves.

It was an effort to recapture runaway slaves living among the Seminoles that set off the first Seminole War. General Andrew Jackson was sent to Florida with a force of some 3000 soldiers to punish the Seminoles.

After destroying several native settlements Jackson succeeded in capturing the Spanish fort at Pensacola in May of 1818, but he did not successfully wipe out Seminole opposition. It would take two additional Seminole Wars to accomplish this.

The next encounter occurred when the Seminole refused to leave under the terms of the Treaty of Payne's Landing in 1832. Two years later, some of the Indians had indeed departed, but the larger segment, led by Chief Osceola refused to go. He was captured and imprisoned for a brief period of time.

Released, he resumed his opposition. He killed the Indian Agent Wiley Thompson. On the same day, Major Francis Dade and his troops were ambushed by 300 Seminole warriors near Fort King, touching off the Second Seminole War. The Indians retreated into the Everglades and engaged in vicious guerilla warfare for the next seven years.

In 1837, in what appeared to be a truce agreement, Osceola was taken prisoner and in 1838 died, but his warriors fought on until 1842 when most had been killed and a little over 4000 surrendered and were deported to Indian Territory in Oklahoma. A remnant of several hundred remained in the everglades under the leadership of Chief Billy Bowlegs.

Chief Bowlegs continued to survive on his land in south Florida until a U.S. surveying crew under Colonel Harney encroached upon his lucrative banana plantation and destroyed the crop. Aroused and angered the chief renewed his guerilla-type attacks on the Americans.

Relentless U.S. skirmishes, assisted by bloodhounds, reduced the number of Seminole Indians to only a couple hundred. Chief Bowlegs surrendered in 1858 and agreed to leave Florida with about 40 of his warriors. Colonel Loomis announced the end of hostilities in Florida.

In northern Illinois and south western Wisconsin, the Sac and Fox Indians had been driven from the area under a disputed treaty signed in St. Louis in 1804, and they were now living in the Iowa territory. Spurred on by chief Black Hawk, they determined to return to their native land across the Mississippi river.

Their return, however, caused the white settlers a great deal of fear and unrest and the governor of Illinois immediately called up the militia. At first it was difficult for the military to find the unwelcome home comers, but finally they did locate them and engaged them in a major battle at Wisconsin Heights, before finally defeating them at Bad Axe on the Mississippi River. This was the last of serious Indian trouble in this area.

West of the Mississippi

Lakota warriors, had fought alongside the British during the Revolution and again in the War of 1812, and in 1815 an agreement was reached which, along with an additional treaty in 1825, gave the Lakota control of a great deal of land, including the areas which today make up the states of Missouri, Iowa, Wyoming, the Dakotas, Minnesota and Wisconsin.

The U.S. government purchased all the land east of the Mississippi which belonged to the Sioux. It would seem that a peaceful conclusion had been reached, but the desire to go west on the part of the white settlers caused them to encroach on the Sioux lands once again and trouble erupted.

No agreement could be trusted. Skirmishes became more frequent. One incident led to another. In 1862, Chief Little Crow led an insurrection in Minnesota, killing hundreds of settlers in the New Ulm area. The U.S. Army responded and the Indians were overwhelmed.

Some of the survivors joined with Oglala tribesmen and under the leadership of Red Cloud and other strong leaders, the white invaders were kept out of their lands for a while. A major conflict, known as Red Cloud's War took place between 1866 & 1867.

Once again superior numbers and firepower prevailed and the conflict ended with a guarantee by the United States of permanent possession of the Black Hills of South Dakota by the Indians. But again the desire of the westward moving settlers, this time led by prospectors anxious to search for gold in the area, caused the treaty to be worthless.

The U.S. commander, Brigadier General George Crook, ordered the Hunkpapa Indians to move onto a reservation. Enraged by this latest assault, Sitting Bull, their chief and Crazy Horse, chief of the Oglala Indians refused to move. Sitting Bull declared that if the soldiers wanted war, he would see that they got it.

In late 1875 a combined force of Indians defiantly left their reservations angered by the continued incursions of white prospectors under the protection given them by the army in contradiction to the official agreements with the U.S. government which supposedly guaranteed Indian privacy and freedom from such violations.

Brigadier General George Crook had placed over a thousand of his men along with 260 Crow and Shoshone scouts north in the Rosebud

Valley in Montana Territory as a result of reports from his scouts that a large concentration of Oglala, Hunkpapa and Cheyenne Indians were located there. He was there to force the Indians back to their reservations.

On June 17, 1876, Crazy Horse and his warriors surprised the army of General Crook and battled them to a standstill in the Battle of the Rosebud. It was one of the largest battles of the Indian Wars. Crook's men withdrew to their base camp in Wyoming.

It is thought by some that this action and the failure of General Crook to rout the Indians had a disastrous impact on the action which followed at the battle of Little Big Horn.

Lieutenant Colonel George Armstrong Custer with a force of over 300 soldiers was a part of a larger force under General Alfred Terry. This is one of the best known of the Indian battles. It has been the focus of many stories and films. It was a fight to the finish between Indians under the leadership of Sitting Bull and the 7th Calvary of the United States Army which began when Custer's men arrived on an overlook about fourteen miles east of the Little Bighorn River.

The rest of the larger force under General Alfred Terry had continued toward the mouth of the river to block any retreat by the Indians. Two friendly Crow Indians were sent ahead as scouts to survey the situation. They reported that a very large encampment was located at the river's edge.

Believing that the Indians were preparing to flee, Custer divided his men into four units and commenced his attack. The first battalion, led by Major Marcus Reno, prepared to attack the southern-most end of the Indian village. Immediately he realized that the enemy was of much greater size than originally expected and that they showed no signs of fleeing. He sent word to Custer requesting reinforcements.

Receiving no response he opened the attack, but fearing that his men might become trapped, he ordered them to fire on the village from a distance. After a long period of time with no sign of relief from Custer, he ordered a retreat into the woods and brush along the river.

The Indians pursued and the battalion fled, moving up the hills to the bluffs which were located east of the river. Here they were met by a squadron commanded by Captain Frederick Benteen who had been sent by Custer to cut off any Indian escape attempts. Their arrival kept Reno's men from being entirely destroyed.

Custer's plan was to attack the northern end of the encampment at the same time that Reno attacked from the south, but he did not figure on the difficulty in maneuvering over the terrain, climbing the hills and dipping through the intervening ravines that lay between his beginning approach and the place where the attack itself could take place.

The Indians were able to concentrate the majority of their forces on Custer and he was too far advanced for reinforcements to rescue him. Custer and his entire force were eliminated. Reno and Benteen joined together in a defensive maneuver on the high ground.

The Indians scattered in small bands to escape being caught. Some were nonetheless captured, while others escaped and fled into Canada along with Sitting Bull. The mighty chieftain later returned to South Dakota and was residing on the Standing Rock Reservation. Brigadier General Nelson A. Miles was afraid that there might be another confrontation and so ordered the capture of Sitting Bull.

It was reported that he resisted arrest and was killed.

The Navajo Indians lived in the area between the Little Colorado and San Juan Rivers in northern Arizona. They were nomadic and frequently attacked Pueblo settlements and later both Spanish and Mexican settlers as well. After the United States signed the treaty of Guadalupe Hidalgo concluding the Mexican War, the U.S acquired the territories of Texas, New Mexico, Colorado, Arizona, Utah, Nevada, California and the Navajo nation.

In 1851, Fort Defiance was built in Navajo territory to control the Navajo Indians and encourage Anglo-American settlement. They attempted to put the Navajo Indians on a reservation but the natives refused to go. When Navajo Chieftain Manuelito found 60 of his livestock killed by American soldiers, he complained to the commander at Fort Defiance and declared that the land belonged to him and not the U.S. soldiers.

In response, a detachment of soldiers and about 160 Zuni warriors set the Navajo chief's fields and his village on fire. Angered, the chief determined to drive the soldiers off his land. He assembled nearly 1000 warriors and attacked Fort Defiance. He nearly succeeded but finally, because of superior gunfire and the defensive structure of the fort, he was forced to retreat.

Under newly arrived American hero, Kit Carson a full scale war was waged against the Navajo. Under Carson's scorched earth policy, the troops killed livestock, poisoned wells, burned crops and orchards, destroyed homes and other buildings forcing the inhabitants to flee. Thousands took refuge in the Canyon de Chelly. That winter, Carson's men erected a blockade at the canyon's entrance and shot at anyone trying to get out. By spring, he rounded up nearly eight thousand starving Indians.

These along with others that had been captured were forced to walk to a reservation at Fort Sumter in New Mexico. The Indians refer to this forced march in a spring blizzard as the "Long Walk". Many died on the way or were killed by the soldiers.

They remained there for four years through harsh winters and crop failures due to bad soil until a new treaty allowed them to move to a reservation established at Four Corners, where four states intersect (Arizona, New Mexico, Utah and Colorado). They were provided with cattle and sheep in return for an agreement to live at peace with the white settlers.

Like the Navajo, the Apache lived in the southwestern area of the country and after the Mexican War ended, the United States stepped up its pressure on the Apache Indians, seeking to place them on reservations. The Apache, like the Navajo, were warlike and resisted fiercely. Found predominantly in the areas of Texas, New Mexico and Arizona the natives fought under the fierce leaders Geronimo, Cochise, Mangas, Coloradas and Victorio.

During the Civil War when many of the frontier outposts were abandoned, the determined Apache led attack after attack on the white settlements. In one instance in 1885 about a dozen braves escaped from a reservation and in a month's time, journeyed over 1,200 miles on horseback. During that time they killed 40 of the white settlers and stole over 200 mules and horses. U.S. soldiers pursued them but were unable to keep them from escaping into Mexico.

The government issued orders to kill every Indian man able to bear arms and capture the women and children. Although the result was to eliminate most of the combatants, some survived, surrendered and agreed to return to the reservation, while other small bands continued to harass the settlers until well into the twentieth century.

An article from the October 12, 1885 New York Times reported local action in Arizona and New Mexico. "It has been recently telegraphed that the pioneer settlers in the border counties of Arizona have brought to light an old law in several counties offering a reward of $250 each for Indian scalps. Under this law, which is nothing more than an order made by the County Commissioners, the ranchmen in Cochise, Pima and Yavapai Counties are organizing in armed bodies for the purpose of going on a real old-fashioned Indian hunt, and they propose to bring back scalps and obtain the reward. Word now comes from Tombstone, the county seat of Cochise County, the reward in that county has been increased to $500 for a buck Indian's scalp. The authorities of Pima and Yavapai Counties have taken steps to increase the reward to $500, and it is said Yuma, Apache and Maricopa Counties will follow suit."

In Utah it was the Ute nation that rose against the onslaught of Mormons. The newcomers were relentless in their invasion, overtaking the Ute lands and taxing their resources and the wildlife that roamed the area. Sensing that the intrusion was getting worse, a Ute effort took place including attacks on the Mormon settlements. The resulting Walker War caused President Lincoln to issue orders to force them onto the Uintah Valley Reservation.

Subsequent encroachment by the Mormons endangered the virtual survival of the natives and Ute braves rose up in an alliance with others of the Paiute and Navajo tribes to embark upon a campaign to pillage the Mormons across the area. A lengthy struggle ensued which was costly to both sides and ended finally in a peace treaty signed in 1868.

Eleven years later, in Colorado, Indian agent Nathan Meeker arrived on the Ute White River Reservation with a plan to change the horse-loving Utes considered primitive savages into pious farmers. He began his crusade by plowing their pony race track into a field for farming. The Indians responded by killing Meeker, ten employees of the agency, burning the agency to the ground and capturing Meeker's family and holding them captive for two weeks. The cry went up that the Ute's must go and they were forced to sign another treaty and relocate to the Ouray Reservation in Utah.

From 1850-1890, disease and murder reduced the population of California natives by 94%. Local bands of volunteers journeyed about the landscape, killing Indian families and winning praise and earning money from the state.

For the sum of $3 settlers could indenture any Indian for a period of 25 years and the going rate for an Indian scalp was from 50 cents to $5. It is estimated that the state paid out over a million dollars for Indian scalps.

In northern California and southern Oregon the Modoc Indians were fishermen and hunters of water fowl and their homes, which resembled little beehives, were found along the banks of Lost River and the shores of Tule Lake.

As the westward movement made its way into their area, they resisted fiercely, but it cost them dearly. Their numbers were reduced to a mere 250 people. They surrendered their lands to the government and moved to the Klamath Reservation in southern Oregon which yielded barely enough sustenance for the members to survive.

Modoc Chief Kintpuash, also known as Captain Jack, took some of his men back into California in 1870. Attempts to get him to return failed and war followed. U.S. soldiers chased the Indians who took refuge at Tule Lake where the lava beds and caves provided protection from the attacking soldiers. Although without arms of any consequence, the small band of about 150 Indians held out for six months. The frustrated soldiers increased their forces to almost a thousand men. In the ensuing efforts to bring about a settlement, General E. R. S. Canby and Eleazer Thomas were killed.

In 1873 the chief and a much decimated number of only 30 braves surrendered. Captain Jack was hanged along with three of his men. Some of the remaining captives were sent back to Klamath Reservation, while others went to Quapaw Reservation in Oklahoma.

In the early 1800s there were an estimated 60 million buffalo roaming the plains of the new country. In the Southern Plains the Indian tribes depended on the buffalo for just about all their needs. As the white hunters began their pursuit of the valued animals the natives resisted, but without success. In 1867 the Treaty of Medicine Lodge moved the Cheyenne, Arapaho and Kiowa to reservations in Oklahoma and Texas. Without the buffalo, the natives had to depend upon the promises of the government for food. When the government failed to adhere to the terms of the treaty the struggle for survival became extremely difficult.

Some of the braves slipped away and began to attack white settlers and hunters. In June of 1874 an attack on about thirty buffalo hunters, one of whom was Bat Masterton, provoked war.

General William T. Sherman and General Philip Sheridan commanded U. S. infantry and cavalry against the renegades. The battle took place in the Red River Valley of northern Texas. Half-starved and greatly outnumbered, the surviving fighters returned to their reservations and their leaders were imprisoned. By the end of 1875 there were no Indian tribes ranging the southern Plains and most of the buffalo had also been eliminated. The path was cleared for white settlers to move in for ranching and farming.

The Rogue River Treaty was signed near the Table Rocks of the southwest Oregon territory. Originally signed with a simple X by Chief Sam and several other chiefs of the Rogue River Indian Tribe, the treaty turned over two million acres of land suited for settlement to the government for a sum of $60,000, of which an amount of $15,000 had to be paid to settlers for expenses they had incurred.

This treaty was the first in the Oregon Territory to be ratified by the U.S. Senate and signed by President Franklin Pierce in 1855. It established a reservation resulting in impoverished conditions among the natives, ruining the traditional tribal economy and throwing the social system into disarray.

Resentment grew among the natives and finally peace was broken when the Indians under Chief Tecumtum took up positions in the Coast Range and effectively beat back attacks by the army, most notably in the Battle of Hungry Hill. They followed the Rogue River to the Pacific Coast searching for food and were attacked by regular U.S. forces from the south and volunteers from the north. The volunteers attacked natives who had already surrendered to the army.

The followers of Tecumtum ended their resistance at Big Bend on the river. They were relocated to the Siletz and Grande Round reservations west of present day Salem, Oregon, but some were forced to march to the Coast Reservation on the central coast.

Also in the Pacific Northwest was a tribe of the Sahaptin Indians, who were nicknamed the Nez Perce` by the French-Canadian trappers. The Lewis and Clark expedition ran into them in 1805.

In 1877 President Ulysses S. Grant opened their homeland in the Wallowa Valley of Eastern Oregon to settlement for the settlers heading west and in addition demanded that all of the Nez Perce Indians in the area move immediately onto the Lawai Reservation in what is today a section of Idaho.

The Indians resisted and Nez Perce Chief Joseph, described as a well-spoken, dignified man, was chosen to meet and discuss the new orders with Brigadier General Oliver O. Howard, a one-armed veteran of the Civil War.

With almost no discussion at all, the general proceeded to issue a 30 day ultimatum calling for the Indians to comply, or else. With no recourse the Indians departed, but a group of young braves began to attack settlers along the Salmon River. Chief Joseph knew that this would cause trouble and prepared for war.

General Howard assembled a battalion and marched on the main Indian encampment. Three hundred Indian braves won an initial skirmish, but realizing that they were hopelessly outnumbered, they fled with the forces of General Howard in pursuit.

Chief Joseph and about 800 warriors engaged the pursuing soldiers in intermittent battles but were seeking to escape on a route that took them southeast through Montana and then back north across what is today Yellowstone National Park. They traveled more than 1,700 miles, dodging the larger number of soldiers on their trail.

Feeling that they had outdistanced the soldiers, they halted for rest about forty miles short of the Canadian border where they would have been safe. Colonel Nelson A. Miles, who had relieved General Howard, led his troops on a forced march of 160 miles in order to catch up to the fleeing natives and conduct a surprise attack.

After five days of fighting neither side had proven superior, but with his ponies stampeded and word of army reinforcements due to arrive imminently, Chief Joseph decided to call it quits and surrendered. Chief White Bird and several of his followers managed to escape into Canada.

The words of the great Chieftain, spoken upon his surrender, have been recorded and translated as follows: "I am tired of fighting. Our chiefs are killed . . . the old men are all killed . . . It is cold and we have no blankets. The little children are freezing to death. My people, some of them, have run away to the hills and have no blankets, no food, no one knows where they are, perhaps freezing to death. I want time to look for my children and see how many of them I can find. Maybe I shall find them among the dead. Hear me, my chiefs, I am tired, my heart is sick and sad. From where the sun stands, I will fight no more forever."

Although Chief Joseph was assured that his men would be permitted to return to their native land in Oregon, political pressure forced them to go to the Indian country in Oklahoma. After about eight years some were allowed to move to the Lapwai Reservation in Idaho, but Chief Joseph and several of his followers were sent to the Colville Reservation in northeastern Washington. He died there in 1904.

Chief Joseph summed up the terrible plight of the Native American Indian who, in situation after situation, fought to hold back the persistent onslaught of the invading hosts of settlers, reinforced and protected by the U.S. Army, only to come to the sad realization that they were hopelessly outnumbered, outgunned and physically exhausted.

Chapter 6

Atrocities Suffered by the Indians

Wounded Knee

There were no further Indian wars in the area until the Massacre of Wounded Knee in 1890 which was the final battle, albeit a one-sided slaughter by the military, of unsuspecting Indian men, women, children and babies.

In 1888 a phenomenon arose in the American west among some of the Indians. A Paiute holy man named Wovoka from Nevada spoke of a vision that he had had which predicted that the earth would soon perish and then come alive again in a pure, aboriginal state, to be inherited by the Indians, including the dead, in an eternal existence free from suffering.

Indians, however, would have to earn this new life by living harmoniously and honestly, cleansing themselves from evil, especially alcohol. He demanded the practice of prayers, meditation, chanting and especially dancing through which one might briefly die and catch a glimpse of the paradise. It became known as the Ghost Dance.

Kicking Bear made a trip to Nevada to learn more. Enthused, he and Short Bull extended the vision to include the possible elimination of the white man. Ghost Dance Shirts were created which were supposed to protect the Indians against enemy bullets.

White officials became disturbed by this new spiritual fervor and fearing what it might lead to, in December of 1890, banned the Ghost Dance on Lakota reservations. The dances continued, however, and troops were called in to the Pine Ridge and Rosebud Reservations in

South Dakota. They were under the command of General Nelson Miles.

Short Bull and Kicking Bear took their followers to a sheltered area in the northwest corner of the reservation. They were joined by Big Foot and his followers who had been asked by Chief Red Cloud to come to the Pine Ridge reservation to restore order. Miles dispatched Major Whitside and the Seventh Calvary to locate the Indians and he found them on Porcupine Creek, not far from Pine Ridge.

Chief Big Foot was ill with pneumonia and was riding in a wagon. The Indians offered no resistance and were ordered to set up camp five miles west of where they were, at Wounded Knee Creek. Colonel James Forsyth arrived.

He ordered his men, who numbered about 500, to encircle the Indians and put in place four Hotchkiss cannons. There were about 350 Indians, of whom 120 were men with the remainder consisting of women, children and babies.

The next morning the soldiers entered the camp and demanded the surrender of all weapons. A medicine man named Yellow Bird advocated resistance at this point, claiming that the Ghost Shirts would protect the Indians from the soldiers' weapons.

One of the soldiers attempted to disarm a deaf Indian and a scuffle ensued. A weapon discharged and other shots were fired by the soldiers. When the Indians ran to seek cover, they were fired upon by the artillery killing at least 150 Indians, including women and children and fifty more were wounded. Forsyth was charged with killing innocent Indians, but subsequently exonerated.

Recognizing that war is always accompanied by suffering, the atrocities inflicted on American Indians went beyond defeating an armed enemy to include devious means to exterminate and totally remove any vestige of his existence.

It is interesting to hear the other side of the story from a descendant of one of the participants in the event at Wounded Knee: "I am Thomas Shortbull and I have been president of Oglala Lakota College for 17 years. My job as president often requires me to differentiate fact from fiction regarding the history of my people, as well as the present quality of life on the Pine Ridge reservation. I would like to take this opportunity to share with you the personal story handed down in my family so that you can better understand, from our perspective, the

1890 Wounded Knee Massacre, a story that has been misunderstood for over a century.

"My Grandpa Shortbull, a spiritual leader, was one of the participants in the spirit or Medicine Dance, mistranslated and called the 'Ghost Dance' by newspaper reporters who deliberately sensationalized a sacred Lakota ceremony to increase newspaper circulation across the country—in other words to make money.

"The Lakota were mourning the deaths of their little children, mothers, fathers and grandparents who had been killed in battles with soldiers. They were trying to live on a reservation without enough food and nowhere to hunt. Malnourishment increased infant mortality and many lost hope that our proud nation would survive. They followed the cultural ceremonies and danced, holding hands in a circle, to produce a vision that would change their lives. Grandpa Shortbull danced with them. False descriptions of the so called "dangerous Ghost Dance" appeared in newspapers telling about hundreds of armed Indians dancing, although no weapons and nothing made of metal was allowed in the Medicine Dance. In less than a month, military officials called in the largest military troop deployment since the Civil War. Thousands of soldiers converged on the small village of Pine Ridge in the middle of winter.

"Chief Spotted Elk (called Chief Big Foot by soldiers) and his band of Minneconjou plus over 30 members of Sitting Bull's Hunkpapa, were called into the Pine Ridge Agency and they began the slow trip to Pine Ridge. Chief Spotted Elk had pneumonia and was bundled up in a wagon so the long caravan of riders and wagons took their time. When they got below Porcupine Bluff, they spotted a military camp and Lakota riders went out to talk with them. The soldiers told them to pitch their tents on the west side of Wounded Knee Creek.

"Exhausted from their long trip, most of the women and children were glad to set up camp and they slept that night. Early the next morning, on December 29, 1890, 500 soldiers surrounded the band of over 300 innocent people, mostly women and children, and began to disarm the men. A disagreement began, a shot was fired and a soldier yelled, 'Fire men! Fire!' the soldiers of Gorge Armstrong Custer's old regiment, the US 7th Calvary, used 4 Mountain Howitzers and hundreds of rifles to slaughter the terrified women, little children and elderly people who could not run away. The Lakota men grabbed rifles from the piles of guns that had been taken from them and they fought back, but it was too late. A blizzard set in that lasted all night, but many dying Lakota were carried off the killing field to die in the camps of their relatives. They were not counted among the dead buried 4 days later in a mass burial, without services of any kind. Soldiers stripped their bodies and auctioned off baby moccasins and Ghost Dance clothing for souvenirs.

"Fifteen years later when Grandpa Shortbull was interviewed about the "Ghost Dance," he said: 'Who would have thought that dancing would have made such trouble? We had no thought of fighting . . . the message that I brought was peace.'"

The Great Cherokee Children Massacre

On August 12, 2006 a memorial was dedicated at Yahoo Falls in McCreary County, Kentucky to the "many innocent women and children who knew no wrong and were massacred by Indian fighters on August 10, 1810."

This was the date when the Great Cherokee Children Massacre took place at Yahoo Falls in southeast Kentucky. The families had been encouraged to bring their children to Yahoo Falls for a journey to Reverend Gideon Blackburn's Presbyterian Indian School at Sequatchie Valley outside of Chattanooga, Tennessee for safety.

They were fleeing from the threat of Indian fighters led by "Big Tooth" Gregory who came from the settlement at Franklin in Sullivan County, Tennessee and had fought under John Seveir. The group's battle cry was "nits make lice," which indicated that nits (baby lice) grew up to be adult lice. They targeted women, pregnant women and children of all ages in their campaigns against the natives.

Big Tooth learned of this pilgrimage and, breaking a peace treaty arranged by Chief Peter Troxell and the Governor of Kentucky, led his followers into Kentucky. After overtaking and scalping a small group of guards, they surrounded and began firing down on the women and children. A bitter battle ensued between the small group of warriors and those of the party able to even attempt to defend themselves, some of whom were armed only with rocks to throw.

The Indian fighters killed the defenders, raped the women and smaller female children of all ages, pillaged, cut bellies open, murdered and scalped over 100 Chickamaugan Cherokee women and children that had been trapped under the falls, killing most of them as they ran begging, huddled together and screaming and pleading for their lives.

The Trail of Tears

This was the relocation of members of the Cherokee, Creek, Seminole and Choctaw nations, among others, from their homelands to Indian Territory in the western United States. The Choctaw were the first to be removed in 1831, followed by the Seminole in 1832, the Creek in 1834, the Chickasaw in 1837 and finally the Cherokee in 1838.

It was the Choctaw Chief, George W. Harkins who was quoted as saying that the removal was a "trail of tears and death." He had previously addressed the American people, saying "We as Choctaws rather chose to suffer and be free, than live under the degrading influence of laws, which our voice could not be heard in their formation."

In the winter of 1838 the Cherokee began the thousand mile march to Oklahoma with scant clothing and most of them with no moccasins or shoes. They had been given some used blankets from a hospital in Tennessee where there had been a small pox epidemic. Because of this, they were prohibited from going into any towns along the way which meant traveling even further.

It was about the third of December when they reached southern Illinois and they were charged a dollar a person to cross the river on "Berry's Ferry". The customary price was only twelve cents. Even then, they were denied passage until all other individuals wishing to cross had been taken care of. Many died while waiting to cross over. Several others were murdered by local settlers. Of the original 15,000 Cherokee who started out, over 4,000 died from disease, the cold, starvation and fatigue.

It would seem that the dislocation of the Cherokee was the most surprising and inconsistent action of the entire period of government versus the Indians. From the days of George Washington, the stated goal of the officials was a desire to civilize the "savages." The Cherokee nation had conformed to their wishes, giving up their culture and native way of life to embrace that of the white man. They were the first and most successful at adopting the dress, culture and tools of the Europeans.

Repeatedly they reinforced government troops in battles with other tribes and they sought through treaties to resolve their differences. In a treaty completed in 1791 between the United States and the Cherokee nation, in the 7th Article, the United States agreed to "solemnly guaranty to the Cherokee nation, all their lands not hereby ceded to the United States."

In another treaty signed in 1798 at Tellico, in the 6th Article, the United States agreed to the guaranty of the remainder of their country forever. These treaties were ratified by President George Washington and the United States Senate.

Further recognition of this position was assured by laws passed by Congress and approved by President Thomas Jefferson in 1802 stating that all persons are prohibited from making any intrusions upon, or surveying the Indian lands secured by treaty.

When the state of Georgia in 1802 passed legislation which insisted on the removal of the Indians from Georgia in violation of federal agreements, the issue eventually went to the United States Supreme Court which ruled in favor of the Indians. President Andrew Jackson, however, chose to disregard this ruling and employed federal troops to remove the Cherokee under the 1830 Indian Removal Act.

Unfortunately, this practice of disregarding agreements and treaties made in good conscience foretold a continued disgraceful pattern of dishonesty and deceit designed to destroy and diminish the Native American Indian population and culture. In some instances it even involved shenanigans through the Indian Agency and their power to appoint temporary chiefs for the sole purpose of signing treaties granting conditions which the government wanted.

The Fort Jones Massacre

In 1851 the Shasta nation made a treaty with the United States government, although never ratified by Congress. The Indians believed it to be in force and when they were invited to a feast to celebrate the occasion at Fort Jones, they accepted the invitation. The meat served was poisoned with strychnine and 4,000 Indians died.

The Bear River Massacre

On January 29, 1863 a peaceful camp of Shoshone Indians was attacked by Colonel Patrick Edward O'Connor. The Bear River Camp was in Washington territory and the Colonel, who was sent to protect pony express riders and the telegraph lines, commanded a force of untrained militia who were prone to excessive drinking.

The assault occurred at dawn and only deep snow prevented the Colonel from employing the howitzers which he had intended to use in the attack. Instead, 55,000 bullets were used to destroy the 300 or so occupants.

As in other such massacres, the arms and legs of the women were broken to keep them from fighting back while being raped. Bayonets were used to cut open wombs of the pregnant so that the fetus could be pulled put. Some of the soldiers then wrapped them around their hats as trophies. After raping the women, they bashed in their heads with hatchets. Babies and toddlers were grabbed and their heads were crushed against tree trunks.

Chief Bear Hunter was beaten, kicked, stripped and whipped until his body was bloody. When he didn't cry out a soldier heated his bayonet and passed it through his ears.

The Colonel then let his men loot the village, taking anything they could find. What remained was set on fire, including food. Another military victory had been recorded.

The Sand Creek Massacre

The governor of Colorado wanted to open the lands occupied by the Cheyenne and Arapaho Indians so white men could settle there. The lands were valuable to the Indians for hunting and they refused to sell and move to a reservation.

During the years between 1850 and 1860 there was tremendous growth in the area. Discovery of gold and silver had caused a rush into the mineral fields, pushing the Indians out. The Pike's Peak Gold Rush brought things to a boiling point.

Governor Evans decided to use force. He used incidents of violence as an excuse to use the military even though they were only isolated events. He called upon Colonel John Chivington, an ambitious Indian-hating soldier who used mostly volunteer men to form a militia.

It was 1864 and the Civil War was in full force. Chivington went into high gear and waged a campaign against the Cheyenne and their allies. Other tribes including the Arapaho, the Hunkpapa, the Oglala, the Comanche and the Kiowa from both Colorado and Kansas joined the Cheyenne in seeking to defend their homes.

A summer of small battles took place before both white and Indian representatives met at Camp Weld, just outside of Denver. No treaties were signed, but it was believed by the Indians that by reporting to the site and camping near army posts, they were seeking peace and expected safety.

Chief Black Kettle was seeking peace along with his band of about 600 Cheyenne and Arapaho followers who followed the buffalo herds along the Arkansas River. In good faith they reported to Fort Lyon and camped about 40 miles north in an area called Sand Creek.

Shortly after their arrival, Colonel Chivington led a force of about 700 militia men into the fort and informed them of his plan to attack the Indian encampment. He was told that the Indians had already surrendered, but he was intent on pressing on with his plan to annihilate more Indians.

On the morning of November 29, 1864 he led an attack force, many of whom had been drinking heavily, and placed them in positions surrounding the Indian encampment. He reinforced them with four howitzer artillery cannons.

Chief Black Kettle, alarmed, but still trusting the Americans, raised both an American flag and a white flag over his teepee. In response, the Colonel gave the order to attack.

With fire from both the big guns and rifles landing on them, the Indians scattered. The crazed soldiers charged, killing anything that moved. The resultant conflict was described as being heartless. "The Indians were scalped, their brains knocked out; the men used their knives, ripped open women, clubbed little children, knocked them in the head with their rifle butts, beat their brains out, mutilated their bodies in every sense of the word." More than 200 Indians had been killed with at least half of that number consisting of women and children.

As a result, Chivington was eventually reprimanded and forced to resign, but the event enraged the other Indians and caused them to resist with greater determination, extending the overall conflict for another twenty-five years.

The Incident at Fort Robinson, Nebraska

"At dusk on January 9, 1879, a young man stood up to rally his people. 'It is better to die fighting than starve to death like dogs! We are Cheyenne!' U.S. soldiers had locked Chief Dull Knife and his band, most of them women, children and elderly in a log building at Fort Robinson, Nebraska Territory. For many days they waited without water, food or heat of any kind. You can imagine how the old people, the pregnant mothers and little children suffered in the crowded barracks. Children licked the snow on the inside of window ledges to find relief from their terrible thirst.

"After the rally cry, the Cheyenne broke out of the windows and ran in the snow. Most were shot down and others chased for miles and killed. Mothers ran with children on their backs and dug a hole, hoping that if they crawled in with their children, they could hide until the soldiers passed by.

But the troopers discovered the hole and ordered that those inside send out the children so that they would be spared. One by one the confused and frightened children climbed out and stood for moment, facing their enemies. Then the innocent children, holding infant brothers and sisters, were slaughtered at close range. The soldiers took positions above the opening and fired round after round until the screaming stopped forever.

"I first heard this terrible story in 1954 when I first came to the Northern Cheyenne Reservation fresh out of a Wisconsin seminary. I was shocked to find these Montana Indians sick, forgotten and living in despair in wall tents and cardboard lined shacks and log cabins with dirt floors, during winter temperatures of 40 degrees below zero."
Father Emmett Hoffman. Founder, Soaring Eagle Living Center.

Brainwashing and Boarding Schools

18   PUNCH, OR THE LONDON CHARIVARI.   [JULY 16 1887.

DEVELOPMENT OF SPECIES UNDER CIVILISATION.
'Arriet. "Ow, 'Arry! I s'y! H'yn't 'e a Ugly Cowve!"

On November 1, 1878, Army Captain Richard H. Pratt opened the Carlisle Indian School in Pennsylvania at an abandoned military post. He had previously been in charge of 72 Apache prisoners being held at Fort Marion, near St. Augustine, Florida. The prisoners were suspected of killing white settlers, but the charges were never proved.

Captain Pratt started a prison school and when the prisoners were eventually allowed to return home he convinced 22 of them to continue their schooling. Several of them were accepted into the Hampton Institute, a school for freed slaves in Virginia. Captain Pratt was a military officer and not an educator, but he had strong opinions about the value of education. He took his ideas from the prison camp with him and opened the Carlisle Indian School.

Upon the opening of the Carlisle School he resigned his Army commission in order to give full time to his new venture. He wanted to bring American Indian children into European culture. In order to achieve his goal he applied the same tactics that cult leaders use to brainwash recruits into following an entirely new way of thinking. His expressed intention was to "kill the Indian, not the child."

With the opening of the Carlisle School, boarding schools became the policy of the government, choosing re-education to extermination as the lesser of two evils.

Most of the schools were run by church organizations. Attendance was compulsory and most followed the mind-control model set forth by Pratt.

Indian children were removed from their reservations and separated from their parents, sometimes for a year at a time and often with no family visits permitted. Uniforms were worn and marching was a pre requisite. Rules were plentiful and punishment swift. The children were forbidden to speak their native language or practice their religion. They were required to memorize Bible verses and the Lord's Prayer.

The students had little privacy and their days were filled with so many required duties that they had little time to think about anything else. Students were expected to spy on each other and report violations to the administrators and teachers.

They were told that the Indian way of life was savage and inferior to the civilized ways of the white man. Indian people who continued in their culture were classified as stupid, dirty and backwards. Those who changed were considered good Indians, while those who did not were thought to be bad Indians. The children were humiliated if they showed evidence of being homesick.

More than 100,000 American Indian children attended the 500 boarding schools that were established following the opening of the Carlisle School. By the 1930s most of the off reservation schools had been closed, but many of the children still attended boarding schools located on the reservations which were operated by missionaries and the Bureau of Indian Affairs. Unfortunately many still retained the discipline and the goal of remaking the students.

This policy, like most of the policies exercised by the United States government in their relationships with the Native American Indians, has caused deep rooted problems for these people. One of the most hurtful of all goals is the turning of children from their parents. For those who wish to cause change it is the chosen way to influence the next generation and is not used exclusively with the Native American Indians, but has found its way into our public school system today.

Joseph Gone, a psychology professor at the University of Michigan in Ann Arbor has described the after effects of the boarding schools as "the cumulative effects of these historical experiences across gender and generation on tribal communities today."

Native American Bar Association President Richard Monette attended a boarding school in North Dakota. He recalls "Learning the fine art of standing in line, single-file, for hours without moving a hair as a lesson in discipline; where our best and brightest earned graduation certificates for homemaking and masonry; where the sharp rules of immaculate living were instilled through blistered hands and knees on the floor with scouring toothbrushes; where mouths were scrubbed with lye and chlorine solutions for uttering Native words."

Both church schools and those run by the Bureau of Indian affairs ran on minimal budgets. Large numbers of children reportedly died of starvation and disease because of inadequate medical attention. Children were routinely made to work at summer jobs to raise money for staff salaries and many were leased out to white families to farm or serve as domestics.

Physical hardship was merely the tip of the ice berg of the systematic assault that was waged on these children. Native scholars have described the destruction of their culture as a "soul wound" from which Native American Indians have still not healed.

Joseph Gone describes a history of "unmonitored and unchecked physical and sexual aggression perpetrated by school officials against a vulnerable and institutionalized population."

Rampant sexual abuse at reservation schools continued until the end of the 1980s, in part because of a loophole in state and federal reporting of allegations of child sexual abuse. In 1987 the FBI found evidence that John Boone (a teacher at the Hopi Indian School in Arizona run by the Bureau of Indian Affairs) had sexually abused 142 boys during the period from 1979 until he was arrested in 1987. The principal of the school failed to investigate a single allegation of abuse.

Boone was found guilty of child abuse and sentenced to life imprisonment. Acting Bureau Chief William Ragsdale admitted that the agency had been lax in following up allegations of abuse and apologized to the Hopi Indians. But the long range damage to the children continues to affect life in the Indian communities even today.

Some of the Hopi Indians testified at a Senate hearing in 1989 that some of Boone's victims had become sex abusers themselves, while others had become suicidal or alcoholic.

Before the influence of the European invaders Native American women were held on a pedestal and violence against women, children and the elders was virtually non-existent. Today, sexual abuse and violence have reached epidemic proportions along with alcoholism and suicide on Indian reservations.

The poisoning of the meat at Fort Jones in 1851 was quick and over with. The impact of the mistreatment and abuse at the hands of those who ran the boarding schools was more widespread and longer lasting.

Canada imported the model for boarding schools in 1880 and continued it in operation well into the 1970s. A 2001 report by the Truth Commission into Genocide in Canada documents the responsibility of the Roman Catholic Church, the United Church of Canada, the Anglican Church of Canada and the Canadian government in the deaths of more than 50,000 Native children in the Canadian residential school system.

The report charges that church officials killed children by beating, poisoning, electric shock, starvation, prolonged exposure to sub-zero weather while naked, and medical experimentation including removal of organs and radiation exposure.

Alberta passed legislation allowing school officials to forcibly sterilize Native girls and British Columbia did the same in 1933. When police began investigating in 1955, hospital staff members destroyed their records. The report also accuses clergy, police and business and government officials of renting out children from residential schools to pedophile rings.

Thousands of survivors and relatives have filed lawsuits against Canadian churches and the government since the 1990s with the cost of settlements estimated at more than $1billion. Many other cases are working their way through the system.

Members of the Boarding School Healing Project say that current levels of violence and dysfunction in Native communities result from abuses perpetrated by state policy. This coalition of activists is using a human rights framework to demand accountability from Washington and the churches involved, in addition to setting up hotlines and healing services for survivors.

We need to understand that many of the violations that have occurred among Native American Indians today are the consequence of human rights violations caused by the abusers rather than an issue of community dysfunction or individual failings.

Chapter 7

Contributions of the Native American Indians

It is amazing that throughout the history of the United States, Native American Indians have continued to stand for the land they love. In spite of broken treaties, forced removal from their original homes onto reservations that are harsh and desolate and even the experience of the white man's boarding schools, they have quietly served our nation.

They helped the Pilgrims survive the harsh and unforgiving conditions of that first winter in the New World. We still remember them at Thanksgiving. Their assistance at Jamestown was invaluable and Pocahontas was able to bring temporary peace between her people and the settlers.

Less well known is the influence of the Great Binding Law of the Iroquois Confederacy. Had the Iroquois not decided to fight on the side of the British against the French, we would all be speaking French now. Additionally, the colonial leaders who were striving to attain independence, unity and democracy were unable to find a model to follow anywhere in the governments of their time.

Europe was engulfed in the rule of monarchs and the authority of the Divine Right of the King. Yet existing right beside them was an example of a successful democratic confederation that had survived for centuries, held together by the Great Law. The colonists witnessed a freedom among the American Indians not found in any European nation.

James Madison made frequent visits to study and speak with Iroquois leaders. William Livingston could speak Mohawk and spent a great deal of time with Indians. Social visits by John Adams and his family with Cayuga chiefs were engaged in frequently. Evidence of Iroquois forms of governance was found among Jefferson's personal papers and Ben Franklin wrote a great deal about Indians and their ideas about freedom and their forms of government.

In 1754 when colonial leaders met in Albany to create the Albany Plan of Union, forty-two members of the Iroquois Grand Council were invited to serve as advisors on confederate structure. Franklin advanced his interest in the Iroquois accomplishment in a speech at the Albany Congress: "It would be a strange thing if six nations of ignorant savages should be capable of forming such a union and be able to execute it in such a manner that it has subsisted for ages and appears indissoluble, and yet that a like union should be impractical for ten or a dozen English colonies."

According to Professor Donald Grinde Jr. of the University of California, Franklin held several meetings with Iroquois chiefs and congressional delegates in order to "hammer out a plan that he acknowledged to be similar to the Iroquois Confederacy." Franklin was present at a meeting of Iroquois chiefs in Lancaster, Pennsylvania in 1774 at which time the chiefs recommended that the colonists stop fighting among themselves and form a union.

It now appears that Iroquois Indians were at the Continental Congress on the eve of the Declaration of Independence. John Adams was advocating the study of Indian governments and he reportedly had observed others among the founding fathers advancing Indian ideas. Somehow historians found it more convenient to overlook this in reporting the birth of our nation.

There are several similar provisions in the Great Law and our Constitution which include the establishment of a federation with separate powers for federal and state governments, provisions for the common defense, representative democracy at the federal and local levels, separate legislative branches that debate issues and reconcile disagreements, checks and balances against excessive powers, rights of popular nomination, recall, and universal suffrage.

Missing from our Constitution, the absence of an executive branch was a solid feature in the Great Law. The Indians had no rulers or presidents. They had a temporary "speaker' who was appointed for one day. The break from the idea of a monarch was too great for the colonists. Likewise, the power to appoint and recall rested with the women in Indian law. It took 150 years after the adoption of the U.S. Constitution before women were even given the right to vote in this country.

And finally, the principle of consensual decision-making was replaced with majority rule. When decisions are made according to a majority vote, potential enemies are made among the losing minority. Certainly disappointment and resentment are present.

When Thomas Jefferson dispatched the Corps of Discovery to explore the vast Louisiana Purchase headed by Meriwether Lewis and William Clark, the expedition faced many challenges because of their lack of knowledge of the geography of the territory through which they would be traveling. Native American Indians helped them find their way and reach their objective.

Lewis and Clark set out with little knowledge of what to expect, believing in fact that there was an easy water route by which they could reach the Pacific Ocean. The original departure was from Pittsburgh, but the expedition began officially at the Missouri River which they followed through what is now Kansas City, Missouri, and Omaha, Nebraska, finally reaching the Great Plains.

It was here that they were assisted by the friendly Mandan and Hidatsa tribes. They proceeded to North Dakota into Nez Perce Indian territory where they were once again helped by the Indians. They acquired the French-Canadian fur trader, Toussaint Charboneau, and his wife, Sacagawea, a Shoshone Indian, who translated and sometimes acted as guide for the explorers. Her presence kept them from appearing as a warring party and saved them from possible harm in their contact with the several Indian tribes which they encountered along the way.

They continued to follow the Missouri River to its headwater and then crossed the Continental Divide at Limhi Pass. Again choosing the water as a highway, they followed the Clearwater River, the Snake River and finally the Columbia River into what is now Portland Oregon. The Clatsop Indians were there for them at the river's edge to direct them on toward their goal of reaching the Pacific Ocean.

The expedition gathered important information about the people, rivers, the mountains, plants and animals that made up the northwestern part of the North American continent and made a major contribution to the mapping of the area.

Once again, the Native American Indians played a positive role in making it happen.

Throughout the development of our nation, Native American Indians have been enlisted to fight alongside the U.S. Army when it was convenient for the government, but when the need disappeared, so did the acceptance of the natives. Native Americans have served in the U.S. military for over 200 years. George Washington praised them for their bravery at Valley Forge. They have fought in every war in modern history.

Many tribes participated in the War of 1812 and Indians fought for both the North and the South in the Civil War. In 1866, the U.S. Army, recognizing their special ability to move about without being seen, established a special Indian Scouts Unit which was utilized in the battle for the West in the late 1800s and early 1900s.

Indian recruits were obtained from Indian Territory by Teddy Roosevelt's Rough Riders for service in Cuba during the Spanish American War in 1898 and they accompanied General John J. Pershing's forces into Mexico in pursuit of Pancho Villa in 1916.

Estimates put the participation of American Indians in World War I at over 12,000. About 600 Oklahoma Indians, mostly Chicasaw and Cherokee, fought with the 142 Infantry, a part of the Texas-Oklahoma National Guard which saw action in France.

Native Americans have the highest record of military service per capita when compared to any other ethnic group. Over 44,000 served in World War II. During that conflict, many Native American men and women left their reservations to work in ordinance depots, factories and other home front efforts to support the armed forces. They even purchased more than $50 million of war bonds to help finance the war, in addition to giving generously to the Red Cross and other wartime charitable organizations.

The idea for using the Navajo language as a secret code to secure communications in WWII came from Philip Johnston, the son of a missionary to the Navajos. He knew of the search by the military for a code that could withstand all attempts to be deciphered by the Japanese and German forces. Johnston believed the Navajo language was the perfect solution since it is an unwritten language of extreme complexity and its qualities make it unintelligible to anyone without extensive exposure or training.

In May 1942 the first Navajo recruits attended boot camp where they underwent Marine training and fine-tuned their code. After training, their job was to transmit information about tactics, troop movements, orders and other vital battlefield communications over telephones and radios. Their code was never cracked and it was considered an instrumental tool in defeating the Japanese forces in the Pacific theatre.

Major Howard Connor, 5th Marine Division Signal Corps officer, declared: "Were it not for the Navajos, the Marines would not have taken Iwo Jima." Long unrecognized by the general public because of the continued use of their language as a secret military code, the Navajo Code Talkers were finally honored for their contributions at a ceremony in the Pentagon in 1992. Ronald Reagan designated August 14th as National Navajo Code Talkers Day, a day dedicated to all members of the Navajo Nation and to all Native Americans who gave of their special talents and their lives so that others might live.

When the war with Vietnam raged, American Indians once again volunteered and served with distinction. Imbedded in their culture are many individual characteristics which make them excellent soldiers including strength, honor, pride, devotion and wisdom.

Individual Native American Contributors

Charles Alexander Eastman

Born near Redwood Falls, Minnesota, to Jacob Eastman (Many Lightnings), a Wahpeton Sioux, and Mary Nancy Eastman, a mixed-blood Sioux, Charles Eastman was greatly influenced by two of the last bloody conflicts between his people and the advancing white forces.

His mother died while he was still a baby, the youngest of five children, and he was given the name Hakadah ("The Pitiful Last") because of his mother's early death. Because of the Sioux uprising in 1887 his family went to British Columbia where he received excellent training as a hunter and warrior.

He was reclaimed by his father who had been imprisoned for his role in the Indian uprising. His father made him attend the Flandreau Indian School.

Subsequently he studied at Beloit College, Knox College and Dartmouth College where he earned a bachelor's degree in 1887 and then at Boston University where he received his doctorate in 1890.

Eastman was the first Native American Indian physician to serve on the Pine Ridge Reservation where he treated survivors of the Wounded Knee Massacre. It was there also that he met and married Elaine Goodale, a poet, educator and reformer.

He went on to serve with the YMCA and the Bureau of Indian Affairs. He became an authority on Indian concerns and was much in demand in both America and England.

In 1893 he began a career as a published author with the help of his wife. Writing many articles, including ten books, he became famous as America's most distinguished Indian writer. In 1933 he was recognized by the Indian Council Fire, a national organization, with the presentation of its first award for "Most distinguished achievement by an American Indian."

Eastman had made the dramatic transition from the traditional life of a Sioux Indian to the drawing rooms and lecture halls of white America. He was an articulate and accomplished physician. His concern for his fellow Native Americans led him to become a lobbyist for the Santee Sioux Tribe in Washington, D.C.

Eastman provided a bridge to self-respect to the Sioux readers. He was able to present their stories, beliefs and customs in the language of the white man. As a cultural bridge builder, he was remarkable.

His greatest contribution to American writing is his own autobiography in which he describes and preserves many Sioux Indian legends, myths and history.

Will Rogers

In his biography of Will Rogers, Joseph H. Carter wrote, "Will Rogers was first an Indian, a cowboy, then a national figure. He is now a legend." He was born on November 4, 1879 on a large ranch in Oologah in Indian Territory, now known as Oklahoma. His parents, Clement Vann Rogers and Mary Schrimsher, were of Cherokee descent.

Will learned how to use a lasso from a freed slave and he used his knowledge effectively in working with Texas Longhorn cattle on the family ranch. He became so skilled that he could throw three ropes at one time, one looping around the neck of a running horse, another circling the rider and the third coming up from the ground to catch all four legs of the galloping steed. This skill landed him in the Guinness Book of Records.

` Rogers left school in the 10th grade to become a cowboy. In 1902 and 03 he traveled in South Africa with "Texas Jack's Wild West Show." He starred as "The Cherokee Kid" and featured his roping skills. He also toured with the "Wirth Brothers Circus in Australia and New Zealand. In 1904 he was featured in both the St. Louis and New York City World's Fairs.

He began to incorporate wise cracks and jokes into his public appearances which overshadowed his roping skills. He became known as an individual who was very informed and a great philosopher, telling the truth in a manner which everyone could understand.

Will Rogers left a spot in the Ziegfeld Follies in 1918 and had roles in seventy-one movies, beginning in silent films, but making it big when sound entered the picture. In 1934 he was voted the most popular male star in Hollywood.

He entered broadcasting, became a syndicated newspaper columnist and authored six books. His work brought him in contact with Presidents, Congressmen and Kings. He went around the world three times, but it was on a vacation flight to Alaska with an aviator friend, Wiley Post, that his life ended prematurely in 1935 in a crash near Point Barrow, Alaska that killed both men.

Roger's wife, Betty, had a memorial constructed in Claremore, Oklahoma, which was dedicated in 1938 by President Franklin Delano Roosevelt. His humor and devotion to the truth make him a legend of the type much needed in today's world of half-truths and dishonesty.

Jim Thorpe

When one thinks about famous Native American Indians the name of Jim Thorpe comes to mind as does the city named after him in Pennsylvania. He had a very diversified and productive life as an athlete. Thorpe's Native American name was Wathohuck or Bright Path. His father was Hiran P. Thorpe of Irish and Sac and Fox Indian extraction. His mother, Charlotte View, was of Potawatomi and Kickapoo lineage.

He was born on May 28, 1888, near Prague, Oklahoma and began school in the Sac and Fox Indian School near Tecumseh, Oklahoma. At the age of eleven he was sent to the Haskell Indian School near Lawrence, Kansas. At sixteen he was recruited to attend the vocational school for Native Americans, the Carlisle Indian School in Pennsylvania.

His athletic ability first surfaced when he cleared the high jump bar at 5'9" while still dressed in ordinary street clothes. He was invited to join the track team by the legendary Glenn S. "Pop" Warner, who coached both track and football. In the fall he went out for football and made the varsity team.

The Carlisle Indians competed against some of the top collegiate teams, often coming away victorious. Some of their opponents were Chicago, Harvard, Minnesota, Nebraska, Penn, Penn State, Pittsburgh and Syracuse. He made third team, All-American, playing half-back.

The following year he left Carlisle and went to North Carolina, playing baseball in the Eastern Carolina Association for whom he pitched and played first base. He was paid $15 a week. This stint of professional baseball cost him his 1912 amateur Olympic status.

In 1911, at a height of six feet and weighing 185 pounds he was talked into returning to Carlisle where he had a remarkable record. Against Harvard's undefeated team he drop-kicked four field goals, two of which were over forty yards and went on to defeat Harvard by an 18-15 score.

In the two year period between 1911 and 1912 Carlisle lost only two games with a schedule that included Army, Syracuse, Penn, Harvard, Pittsburg and Georgetown. Thorpe scored twenty-five touchdowns and accounted for 198 points. He was named All-American for the second year.

During the summer of 1912 he was chosen to compete in the decathlon and the pentathlon in the Olympics in Stockholm. He won four of the five events in the pentathlon to take that gold and he set a world record in points that remained for over twenty years. Thorpe declared that the receiving of his gold medal in Stockholm was the proudest moment of his life.

Less than a year later, charges of professionalism were brought against him and the American Olympic committee declared him a professional. They asked that his medals be returned and his name was removed from the records. Several attempts to reverse that decision failed until finally, in 1982, William Simon, President of the United States Olympic Committee met with Juan Samaranch, President of the International Olympic Committee and the decision was made to restore his medals.

Following his Olympics experience, Thorpe played professional baseball for the New York Giants, the Cincinnati Reds and the Boston Braves. In his last year in the majors he hit for an average of .327.

He also played professional football and was the chief drawing card for any team for whom he played until the appearance of Red Grange. Thorpe retired in 1929 at the age of 41.

The Associated Press polled sports writers and broadcasters to determine whom they considered the greatest football player and the most outstanding male athlete of the first half of the 20th century. Thorpe won over Red Grange and Bronco Nagurski in the football department and outdistanced Babe Ruth and Jack Dempsey as the outstanding male athlete.

Jim Thorpe joined the Merchant Marine late in World War II. He died in 1953. Shortly after his death, the Boroughs of Mauch and East Mauch Chunk, which are located at the gateway to the Pocono Mountains in Pennsylvania, merged and adopted the name of Jim Thorpe because of his fame and drawing power. After purchasing the remains of the famous athlete from his third wife, they erected a monument to him and began a massive marketing program to attract tourists.

Mauch Chunk derived its name originally from the phrase "sleeping bear" in the language of the native Lenape Indians because of the near-by Bear Mountain (which looked like a sleeping bear). The borough is located in Carbon County, of which it is the county seat. According to the 2000 census it is populated by 4,804 people. It has been called, "the Switzerland of America," because of its picturesque scenery, its location in the mountains and the architecture of its buildings.

Its characteristic architecture contains many 19th century styles including Federalist, Greek Revival, Second Empire, Romanesque Revival, Queen Anne and Richardsonian Romanesque.

Billy Mills

Another famous athlete, Billy Mills, is an Oglala Lakota (Sioux), who was raised on the Pine Ridge Reservation in South Dakota in a four room house of board construction that often sheltered as many as fifteen people. His mother was three-quarters French and one quarter Indian. She died when Billy was quite young. His father was Lakota (Sioux). He too died when Billy was only twelve, leaving the boy an orphan.

He and his sibling were sent to Haskell Indian School where he became involved in running. He would run five or ten miles on weekends to get away from other people because of his great loss of a father he adored.

A graduate of the University of Kansas, which he attended on a track scholarship, he then served as an officer in the United States Marine Corps. On October 14, 1964 he won the 10,000 Meter Run in Tokyo, remaining the only American to ever win the Gold Medal in that event. The Lakota people awarded Warrior Status and an Indian name, Makoce Terila (Respects-the-Earth).

He holds the World Record for the Six Mile Run, held in San Diego in 1965, as well as Seven American Records in Track and Field in that same year. In 1972 he was chosen among the Ten Outstanding young Men of America by the US Jaycees and elected to the United States Olympic Hall of Fame in 1982. He has been elected to five other Halls of Fame.

As the National Spokesman for "Running Strong for American Indian Youth," he travels most of the year, visiting American Indian communities throughout the country and emphasizing to the youth the need for healthy lifestyles and encouraging them to be proud of their heritage. Billy Mills was selected as the "Best Indian Role Model" by the Native Times Reader's Poll, 2000-2001 and 2002-2003.

John Herrington

Born in Wetumka, Oklahoma, in 1958, John Herrington is an enrolled member of the Chickasaw Nation and an American astronaut with one space shuttle mission under his belt. To honor his Native American heritage, he took a Chickasaw Nation flag with him on his space voyage.

He lived in Colorado Springs, in Colorado; Riverton in Wyoming, and Plano in Texas. After graduating from Plano High School, Herrington earned a bachelor's degree from the University of Colorado in Colorado Springs and then was commissioned in the United States Navy in 1984. He received a Master of Science degree in aeronautical engineering from the U.S. Naval Postgraduate School in 1995.

After service in the Pacific he was assigned as a test pilot and subsequently selected as an astronaut candidate in 1996. He flew his first space mission in 2002 as a mission specialist aboard STS-113. He has logged over 3,800 flight hours in over 30 different types of aircraft.

In 2005 Herrington resigned from NASA to become Vice President /Director of Flight Operations for Rocketplane Limited, Inc. He also gives support to the Center for Space Studies at the University of Colorado.

Honored as the Distinguished Naval graduate from Aviation Officer Candidate School in March of 1984, he has also received the Navy Commendation Medal, the Navy Meritorious Unit Commendation, the Coast Guard Meritorious Commendation Medal and several other service related awards.

In 2007 he resigned from Rocketplane Global, Inc. and has been engaged in public speaking appearances and work with the Chickasaw Nation.

. On August 13, 2008 Herrington began a cross-country bicycle trip which started in Cape Flattery, Washington and ended in Cape Canaveral, Florida. The event was called Rocketrek and its purpose was to encourage students to become more interested in math and science. En route he made stops at NASA Explorer schools and Indian reservations to further his special effort.

The Buffalo Nickel

The U. S "Buffalo" or "Indian Head" nickel was minted from 1913 to 1938. The face of the Indian on the coin was a composite of three men selected by designer James Earle Fraser. One was Iron Tail (Sinte Maza) who was an Oglala Indian. He lived from 1850 to 1916 and fought under Sitting Bull at the Battle of Little Big Horn in 1876.

The second was Two Moons (Ishi'eyo). He was a Cheyenne, living from 1847 to 1917, who also fought at the Battle of Little Big Horn. The third was Big Tree who was a Seneca Indian who acted in many silent movies in the 1920's. One of the movies was the "Frontiersman."

On the reverse side of the coin is an American bison called Black Diamond who was living at the time in the Central Park Zoo in New York City. This same design is found on American buffalo 24 karat gold coins as well as buffalo silver dollars.

In 1859 the Indian penny was introduced, depicting an Indian chief's daughter on one side. An interesting story is told which reports that the chief loaned the headdress of his daughter to the designer to have the picture created. Most Indian cents minted during the Civil War went to Union soldiers.

The first and only paper currency with an Indian featured is a five dollar bill which carries the image of Hunkpapa Chief Running Antelope, complete with a Pawnee ceremonial headdress. The use of the substitute headdress was necessary because the chief's Hunkpapa headdress was too tall for the engraving.

Chief Running Antelope was known for his bravery in war and a close advisor to Chief Sitting Bull. The two parted company because Chief Running Antelope believed that compromise with the white man was in the best interest of the Indians.

Several gold coins feature Native American Indians. The $2 ½ dollar Indian gold piece, the $5 Indian gold coin and the $10 Indian gold coin are examples. In addition, the Sacagawea Gold dollar honors the Shoshone wife of the French Canadian fur trapper who helped the Lewis and Clark expedition as interpreter and guide.

Other contributions

American Indians were the first to cultivate over seventy-five percent of the many varieties of food grown in the world today. Vegetables that originated with the Indians constitute a major part of our daily menu. Some of those foods include corn, potatoes, sweet potatoes, peanuts, squash, pumpkins, tomatoes, and many species of beans. We can also thank them for turkeys and honey.

Many of today's medicines were discovered by Indian healers centuries before the European invasion. Such things as quinine, syringes, beef jerky, freeze-dried foods, root beer and rubberized clothing are part of the gifts of the Native Americans.

The colonies had a short supply of money and they borrowed the practice of the Indians in using "wampum" as well as bartering for such items as tobacco, furs, indigo, rice and wheat. Wampum was a string of shell beads, sometimes as long as six feet. The colonists actually manufactured wampum.

The earliest known wampum factory was located in New Jersey in 1760, operated by J.W. Campbell. His factory continued making wampum for a hundred years. As demand increased, new ways were found to make more wampum faster and cheaper. The Campbells were in business for profit. The Indians made wampum to fill a need.

Chapter 8

Conditions on Reservations Today,

According to the September 12, 2002 issue of the Rocky Mountain News more than half of the 2,500,000 American Indians in the country live on reservations located throughout the nation. There are 314 federally recognized reservations, most of which are located in the western United States which occupy 44 million acres of land, most of which offer the poorest quality of soil and are located in areas of harsh climactic conditions. Some include bodies of water.

Tribal and Federal jobs provide the majority of available job opportunities, leaving the unemployed dependent upon welfare and other subsistence programs. Food stamps are of little help because of the lack of stores on the reservations in which to redeem them.

Reservation locations were determined in a number of ways. Some tribes, like the five tribes in the Trail of Tears were forcibly moved to Indian Territory, west of the Mississippi where it was believed white men would never want to go. A few tribes were able to avoid removal and are located on marginal land in their original homelands. For the most part, reservations are located where no one else would choose to locate.

They bear different titles depending upon their location. In California, about half are called Rancherias, while in New Mexico, most reservations are called Pueblos while other Native American areas in that state are called Indian Colonies. Most are simply known as Reservations. To the inhabitants they are often considered concentration camps. They are removed from proximity to any source of income, their natural resources, if any existed, have been depleted and they are for the most part dependent upon the federal government for their sustenance.

Like most of the agreements made by the government the promises have again been broken. The relationship between the Indian nations and the United States of America was established by a decision of the United States Supreme Court in a dispute between the Cherokee nation and the state of Georgia wherein the court ruled that American Indian Tribes were "domestic dependent nations" which has led to the concept that tribes are nations with rights to internal self-government on federally recognized reservations.

That portion of the decision which described them as domestic dependent nations means that the reservations are the direct responsibility of the federal government and are held in trust for the tribes. Even though they have elected legislatures, the tribal government may not sell land without the consent of the federal government. The execution of this federal responsibility is in the hands of the Bureau of Indian Affairs, a division of the Department of the Interior.

According to a recent U.S. News and World Report, "it is not poverty alone that has condemned many American Indians to lives as bleak and hard as the lands where the United States government dumped them a century ago." The headline described the Bureau of Indian Affairs (the agency developed to look after the welfare on Native Americans) as "The Worst Federal Agency . . . a national disgrace."

The American Indian Citizenship Act of 1924 granted dual citizenship to Native American Indians, making them full citizens of the United States and the state in which they live, while remaining citizens of their respective Indian nation.

While this may appear to resolve the problems of the Indians, it in fact further complicates them. In some cases, lack of leadership on the part of the Indians creates trouble which is difficult for outside help to correct. In others, the action or lack of it on the part of the Bureau of Indian Affairs is the culprit. Finally, the politicians recognize that the Indians do not present a strong political force and therefore they do not receive the attention they deserve.

John Kennedy, Bill Clinton and John McCain have all pointed to the disgraceful situation into which our federal government has placed these original inhabitants of our great land, but no one has done anything to change the situation. While the press has occasionally covered some of the shortcomings, such as the situation in California, they have not made it an issue and have dropped the ball in search of news that will sell more papers, attract more listeners or gain more viewers. Or perhaps there may even be hidden reasons.

In the meantime, children continue to suffer, Elders die unnecessarily, abuse runs rampant and innocent people continue to pay a high price for the misconduct of those who have gone before. The situation of the Native American Indian remains an inconvenient skeleton in the closet of a strong, wealthy and "righteous" nation.

The August 18, 2003 edition of the Denver Post reported that the 1,185 acres of the Pine Ridge Reservation include the two poorest counties in the entire United States. The poorest county is Buffalo County, South Dakota, location of the reservation of the Crow Creek Sioux Tribe where nearly 7 out of every 10 people live below the poverty level. The per capita income is only $5,213 a year. The second poorest county is Shannon County in which 52% of the residents (94% Native American Indians) live below the poverty line.

We are the nation which paid with hundreds of thousands of lives to win the right for slaves to be free. We sacrificed for years to defeat the dictator Adolf Hitler in Europe, and then put together the Marshall Plan to rebuild and help Germany recover economically and structurally.

The same nation which, after defeating the tyranny of the Japanese Emperor Hirohito, sent Douglass MacArthur to head an economic recovery plan that lifted the impoverished nation of Japan to a position of leadership in world trade. We organized an air-lift to bring relief to the suffering of the Germans in West Germany behind the Iron Curtain and then stood strong in the Cold War to force the collapse of the Russian threat to world peace. And we sacrificed to rid Iraq of a ruthless dictator and offer freedom to the Iraqi people.

But after three centuries of persecution, out-right hatred and appalling discrimination against them, the American Indians remain in dire poverty. Rusted-out cars and tiny, weather-beaten, homes line the streets. Sometimes two and three families are forced to live in dilapidated dwellings that they call home. There is a shortage of food and water and the brutal winter months and disease will threaten the lives of thousands of vulnerable elders and young children.

Indian Country Today, in a March 10, 2004 publication, reported that only 68% of American Indian households have telephones compared to 95% as a whole for the nation. There are 90,000 homeless or under-housed Indian families and 30% of the existing housing is overcrowded with less than 50% of the homes connected to a public sewer.

The Mdewkanton Shakopee on the Northern Plains are among the richest of all Indian nations, but the Lakota and Oglala in South Dakota are the most impoverished ethnic group in America today, suffering from the highest poverty level and unemployment rate, lowest wages and poorest education.

They struggle daily with isolation, limited employment opportunities and a harsh and resource-poor environment. Poverty is common and places a heavier burden on those who are most fragile—the elderly, the children and extended families.

The remote location and limited resources of many communities, a lack of suitable land and harsh weather conditions contribute directly to the deplorable living conditions found on most reservations. In many instances it is not uncommon to find as many as 25 people living in a two-bedroom house which is substandard and in need of extensive repairs. Almost half of the residences are not connected to a public sewer. The need for adequate housing on reservations is acute.

Winter brings cold weather and deep snow drifts. Nearly every winter the roads to most of the remote Sioux communities in the Badlands become impassable during major storms.

"Congress has slashed funds going to reservations. Government programs intended to help American Indian families are being eliminated or drastically reduced. These are programs that were promised when the federal government made treaties with the Sioux tribes. The Indians gave up their land and their way of life as a result of these treaties," writes *Darwin Long, Chairman, American Indian Relief Council.*

On average, American Indians residing within the borders of Arizona live to be only 54.7 years old. Navajo Indians are four times more likely to have diabetes than non-Navajos. Over 40% of adult Navajo deaths are caused by diabetic complications. The rate of death from tuberculosis for Native Americans is 500% higher than other Americans. The suicide rate among Navajo teens is 4 to 5 times that of U.S. national averages. *Katie Tree, Chairperson Southwest Indian Relief Council.*

Greater than 40 per cent of the families living on reservations do so below the 1999 federal poverty line according to the Arizona Daily Star (May 25, 2002). Because of the scarcity in opportunities for employment, the jobless rate often exceeds 85%. On the Pine Ridge Reservation in South Dakota, residents will walk or hitch rides a distance of forty miles into Rapid City to work at jobs paying as little as $56 a day according to an article in the Washington Times of September 1, 2002.

Often the head of the household will leave the reservation to find work, leaving grandparents to assume the task of raising grandchildren. For reasons of survival, extended families pool their meager resources in their struggle to meet the daily demands of the family members.

The suicide rate on the Cheyenne River Reservation, like that of other Native American Indian reservations, is greater than three times that of the national average for American teenagers. In 2007 the number of students who killed themselves in the first three months of the year equaled that of the entire previous year, causing the Rosebud Sioux Tribe to declare a state of emergency. Two years later the Pine Ridge reservation also found it necessary to do likewise to deal with the suicide problem

59% of the homes on the Rosebud Reservation are substandard and lack water, electricity, adequate insulation and a sewage system. Almost 305 of the people who reside there are homeless. Every winter there are deaths from hypothermia.

The average age of Native American Indians as a whole is 55 years which is lower than that of Bangladesh. The Great Falls Tribune noted in an article published on June 23 of 2002 that the federal government spends only half as much on health programs for each tribal member as it does for other American individuals.

In an encouraging note, Katie Tree who chairs the Southwest Indian Relief Council shares this anecdote in her one of her communications. "Guadalupe, Arizona is a small town of about 6,000. It was founded about the turn of the last century by the Yaqui Indians who were forced to flee their homeland to avoid persecution and enslavement. Over 40% of the community lives below the poverty level and another 35% are considered working poor. Many families are without decent housing and face poor sanitation conditions every day.

"John Molina is of Apache and Yaqui decent. He left his hometown to become a doctor and then returned to help provide health care through the establishment of the Molina Clinic. With the help of the Southwest Indian Relief Council and private financial donors, it provides health care to Yaqui Indians living in Guadalupe without regard to ability to pay."

"The failure of the United States government to honor treaties made with the Indians has left them in devastating conditions. Their will to survive helps them prevail over tremendous odds," says Linwood Tall Bull, Chairman of Native American Aid.

As a direct result of the colonization of the nation over the past two centuries, the daily lifestyle of the Native American Indian has changed dramatically which has had the effect of changing health concerns from primarily infectious disease to more chronic diseases such as diabetes, heart disease and cancer.

Native American Indians are 48.47% more likely to suffer from heart failure, 173% more likely to suffer from diabetes and 44.3% more likely to suffer from asthma than the general population according to the July 11, 2002 issue of the Everett Herald.

Life expectancy on the Pine Ridge Reservation is the lowest in the entire western hemisphere except for Haiti according to the Wall Street Journal. The average family income is $3700 and it is considered to be the most impoverished community in America.

The statistics are unbelievable and obviously the need is great. The problem is complex and efforts to solve it have fallen far short of doing so. Yet we succeeded in putting a man on the moon and solved many health problems which also seemed to have no answers.

As individuals we can respond to the immediate needs of the Native Americans by supporting the charities which are listed in this book's appendix, but we need to go further. We need to look seriously into new alliances that can help to create better understanding and introduce new ways to establish programs that will lift Native American Indians into a new relationship with today's white population based upon our understanding of the all-inclusive meaning of "One nation, under God" and equal opportunity for all peoples.

Chapter 9

The War Goes On

The Indian threat to white settlers has been eliminated, but amazingly, the threat of the white man to the Indian continues. The courts have been, and continue to be, a violent weapon used against Indian people replacing the guns of yesteryear. The idea of an Indian in court is foreign to many of us. The thought of the Cherokee President going to Washington back in the early 1830s to argue peacefully for the rights of his people is foreign to the traditional image of the Native American Indian to which we have become accustomed. It doesn't fit the picture that most of us have from our classrooms and from the dramatic, yet one-sided, projection of the Hollywood directors.

The re-emergence of Indian self-respect over the last several decades has caused serious problems for these native inhabitants, especially in California. This is evidenced by the Alcatraz occupation by Indians of several tribes in 1969; the struggle which is ongoing on the Pitt River reservation; battles between the authorities and the Klamath Indians over fishing rights; the founding of D-Q University; the sawmill struggle involving the Toyon Wintu Indians and the ongoing arguments over the federal refusal to recognize many California Indian tribes.

Consider the plight of the Muwekma Ohlone Tribe of the San Francisco Bay area. Their ancestral history dates back over ten thousand years before their contact with Spanish explorers in 1769. In that year the Bourbon Monarchy of the Spanish empire decided to expand its presence into California and the first of a series of contacts occurred between the Spanish colonial empire and the native Costanoan/Ohlone people living within the territories of Monterey and the San Francisco Bay area.

During the early Spanish expeditions the Spaniards encountered a number of Muwekma Ohlonean tribes and villages. Generally the Indians looked upon strangers in one of two ways: they were either enemies or distinguished visiting guests. According to documented accounts, the Spanish were looked upon as distinguished guests and they were invited into their villages and treated accordingly.

But the intolerant alien order imposed by the conquering Hispanic empire reduced their number from the twenty some thousand that inhabited the area in 1769 to less than 2000 by 1810. Their numbers continued to decline as other tribal groups were displaced or hunted down. Alisal, as well as other Rancherias (reservations) became safe havens for the Muwekma Ohlone tribesmen as well as members from other neighboring tribes with whom they had intermarried.

In the 1880s the Hearst family purchased the land on which the Rancheria was located and allowed the Muwekma living there to remain. During the early part of the twentieth century the Muwekma Ohlone Indians became federally recognized as a result of the Special Indian Census. It was determined that there were about 20,000 Indians left in California, a devastating decline from the more than one and half million who had lived there when the Spanish arrived in 1769.

In 1925 Dr. Alfred L Kroeber of the Anthropology Department at Berkeley published his "Handbook of California Indians," in which he declared the Costanoan group extinct. Somehow, the surviving Costanoan/Ohlone Indians never heard of their extinction and instead continued to maintain their culture and existence.

The United States Government maintained a "Trust" relationship with these tribal groups from 1906 to 1927. At that time they were administratively dropped along with 135 other Acknowledged California Indian communities from their Federally Recognized Status by Lafayette A. Dorrington, Superintendent of the Bureau of Indian Affairs in Sacramento. This action was contrary to Bureau of Indian Affairs policy and done without any notification or due process to the tribes.

Even though they have enrolled with the Bureau of Indian Affairs under the 1928 California Jurisdictional Act, and have organized according to the Bureau's Directives, they are still not recognized as an Indian tribe under federal law. In spite of nearly 13,000 years of human history, they are still trying to recover from the sentence of "extinction" by scholars, politicians and anti-Indian activists.

Eight years after petitioning and the offering of several thousands of historic and legal documents, on May 26, 1996 the Bureau of Indian Affairs Branch of Acknowledgement and Research made a positive determination that they had been previously acknowledged between 1914 and 1927, but they were still required to submit additional documentation and after another two year period they were placed on the ready for the active consideration list as of March 26, 1998.

The Muwekma Tribal Council checked the Federal Register and determined that there were twenty-four other tribes ahead of them on that list. The time schedule for processing tribal petitions was about 1.3 per year, meaning that the earliest that their petition would be considered was over 20 more years.

They did a very civilized thing. They filed a law suit against the Interior Department/Bureau of Indian Affairs. On June 30, 2000 Federal district Judge Ricardo M. Urbina ruled in favor of the Muwekma tribe and ordered the Interior Department to formulate a process to deal with the issues contained in the complaint.

During the period from September to October of the year 2000 the Muwekma Council filed two additional Exhibits and finally the Department of Interior's branch of Acknowledgment and Research Tribal Services Division of the Bureau of Indian Affairs reported them as a "previously recognized tribal entity." But the tribe has yet to advance through the "Recognition Process" for complete reinstatement of its Acknowledged status. Meanwhile its Elders are passing on and the numbers continue to drop.

The Muwekma, and about 40 other California Indian Tribes must continue to endure Bureau of Indian Affairs bureaucratic inertia and obstruction. These natives, who have never left their ancestral homelands, have waited for the United States government to act since 1906, but the government did magnanimously make a token payment of $668.51 (computed with interest from back to 1851) as just compensation for the illegal acquisition of California land, minerals and resources.

For other tribes the ordeal has been equally as difficult. It took the Cowlitz Tribe 22 years to go through the Recognition Process and the Samish Tribe of Washington State had to wait 25 years, which included eight years of litigation. It was found that the Department had denied "Due Process" to the Samish Tribe. Imagine what the consequences might have been if the Bureau of Indian Affairs had not been created to protect and serve the Indians.

Unfortunately this happens frequently. Non-native researchers and "scientists" draw conclusions from sometimes incomplete, sometimes outdated, sometimes obsolete sources and publish their work which leads other people to accept what they say as accurate because it is in print.

It might be appropriate to review the historic relations of treatment of the Natives by the United States government. It is a relationship that has evolved over the centuries as the new country expanded and wrestled with the many problems caused by growth and the administration of the many details of governing.

The first official agency to oversee the terms and promises of treaties signed between the government and the Indians was located in the office of the Secretary of War in the year 1789 when Secretary Henry Knox appointed "peace missionaries" to the Indian tribes in an effort to promote "civilization" among the tribes and to make peaceful relations easier to accomplish.

The name of "Bureau of Indian Affairs" was not officially used until 1796. Many treaties required that an agent live with the tribes. In the early nineteenth century the agents were responsible for overseeing the Indian trading houses and for distributing annual payments to the tribal chiefs.

The situation created a great opportunity for dishonesty on the part of the agents, and while most were honest and efficient, the number of those who were involved in mismanagement and corruption was significant. Agents often had little formal education and government allocations did not clearly define the difference between funds for private use and those for official purposes.

In the years following the Civil War there was a considerable public outcry for more efficiency and humane treatment of the Indians by the agents and the agencies. During the administration of Ulysses S. Grant there was a movement which resulted in the involvement of Christian organizations in controlling the agencies.

Their intention was to improve the agencies, but they failed to do so and by 1882 all of the churches had withdrawn their involvement because there were very few candidates for the job who were both devout Christians and competent administrators.

Beginning in 1880 the duties of the agents were increased to include teaching English to the Indians along with courses in industrial and agricultural arts. But in spite of the requirements, agents continued to be appointed for political reasons rather than because they were qualified. President Grover Cleveland decreed that applicants for the position would have to pass competitive examinations and they were to be included in the civil service system.

The involvement of Indians themselves in these positions was limited to menial tasks and it wasn't until 1934 that a provision in the Indian Reorganization Act afforded the opportunity for Indians to gain employment without taking the civil service test. By 1972 Native Americans held the majority of top-level executive positions in Washington D.C. and also seven of the twelve area superintendent positions.

Within the Office of Indian Affairs is the division of Tribal Government Services. Its mission is to promote awareness of tribal responsibilities, as well as to provide tribes with the resources needed to foster stable tribal governments in exercising their rights as sovereign nations.

Tribal Government Services carries out this policy by supporting and assisting Indian Tribes in the development and maintenance of strong and stable tribal governments capable of administering quality programs and developing economies of their respective communities.

It is appropriate to pause here to remind the reader of the preceding chapter which describes the conditions found on most reservations throughout the country today. It would certainly appear that these words, like so many of the treaties and proclamations of the U.S. government in their historic dealings with the Native American Indians, are hollow at best and fall far short of accomplishing their goal.

Tribal Enrollment also fails to get the job done, because of considerable bureaucratic red tape and the natural delays which are common to the operation of our government, especially when the issue involves a population without political clout. A blood quantum introduced by the white man for registration purposes has been adopted by some Indian organizations for political expediency. It is difficult for many to become officially numbered as part of a tribe and the last resort is the courts, which once again involves a considerable expenditure of time and a large amount of money.

That situation is magnified in the case of tribal claims which can go on for decades without resolution. The cause of protection of sacred sites is a case in hand as well as the mineral rights and even hunting and fishing rights of native tribes where these are in contention with the rights of white individuals or businesses.

Add in the claims which involve specific language existing in Treaties and agreements between the Native American Indians and the government which have been broken by the government related to such things as land, territories, natural resources and self-determination and one can see the frustration and disappointment of the Indians.

The denying, undermining and diminishing of rights promised and considered viable relating to social services, child and family wellness, traditional subsistence, health care, education, culture, spiritual practices and language is a disgrace and it is not difficult to see why there is a great deal of suspicion where relationships with the government are concerned.

It is difficult to rationalize a situation in which we, the people of this great nation, continue to violate and abuse the rights given by God and guaranteed under our Constitution to all people, especially since these special people were granted citizenship in 1924. They are not illegal immigrants who have broken our laws to get here and yet they receive less support than those who have. They are the original inhabitants of this portion of the world whom we have usurped in our desire to gain wealth and power.

Following the War of 1812, during which many of the Indians fought along with the British, the fledgling American nation took upon itself a policy which focused on the removal of the Indians. They decided that the natives should be relocated west of the Mississippi River in the great American Desert because it was thought at that that no white man would ever want to live there.

This time of forced removal started in 1802. The state of Georgia owned a great deal of land west of the Mississippi which it gave to the federal government as a result of an agreement that the federal government would abolish all Indian titles to land within their state. When nothing had happened by the mid-1820s the issue started to fester. The Cherokee Indians held a great deal of land in Georgia which they feared losing. To work within the white man's laws, they adopted a constitution which proclaimed their jurisdiction over all lands in their territory.

By this time the rights of the Indians and the interests of the state of Georgia were in deep contradiction. The Indians had no recourse but the courts, but when they asked for assistance from the newly elected President Andrew Jackson, he refused, saying that he did not want to interfere with the lawful rights of the states. Instead, he proposed legislation that would force the Indians to leave.

In Georgia, legislation was passed which made it illegal for an Indian to bring suit against a white man, encouraging theft and plundering on the part of many white settlers.

President Andrew Jackson, a veteran Indian fighter was given the power in the Indian Removal Act of 1830 to exchange land west of the Mississippi for the desired territory in the East of the "Five civilized Tribes," which included the Cherokee, the Creek, the Choctaw, the Chickasaw and the Seminole.

In spite of a Supreme Court decision which ruled that the Cherokee nation had the right to retain their lands in Georgia, Jackson refused to acknowledge that decision and the Cherokee Indians were forced to make the long trip to Oklahoma in the dead of winter which has become known as the Trail of Tears because of the many who died and because they had to leave both their physical and their spiritual homes. In many cases they had to leave the land they had cultivated without even being able to collect their belongings.

President Jackson made a promise to the Indians of perpetual autonomy in the West. The Five tribes surrendered all of their lands in the east. In exchange they were given 19,525,966 acres which were divided between the five tribes. The Choctaw got 6,953.048 acres in the southwest portion of Oklahoma. West of the Choctaw, the Chickasaw were given 4,707,903 acres. In the northeast the Cherokee received 4,420,068 acres. The Creek obtained 3,079,095 acres located southwest of the Cherokee and sold 365,852 acres to the Seminoles.

Additionally, large sums of money were held in trust by the United States government for each of the tribes. The Cherokee had $2,716,979, the Choctaw $975,258, the Chickasaw $ 206,695, the Creek $2,275,168 and the Seminole $2,070,000. The money was to support the tribal governments and the schools.

President Jackson had this to say about the removal: "It will separate the Indians from their immediate contact with settlements of whites, enable them to pursue happiness in their own way and under their own rude institutions, will retard the progress of decay, which is lessening their numbers, and perhaps cause them to gradually, under the protection of the government and through the influences of good counsels, to cast off their savage habits and become an interesting, civilized and Christian community."

As a result of the many wars which we have previously described, by the end of the 1840s, the Indian problem had been solved in the East. The West, however, was another story entirely and in spite of specific language to the contrary found in agreements repeatedly agreed to by the United States government, the ongoing expansion westward by white settlers caused a continuation of battles.

Forcibly restricted to living on reservations, the displaced natives found it difficult to survive and they became dependent on the government for their survival. The white population of the country was divided. Some believed in the right to ownership and wanted the Indians to own their own farms and become independent farmers. Other felt that the Indians had already been given too much.

The outcome of this pressure led to the passage of the Indian General Allotment Act of 1887. The Act provided that land previously held in common by Indian tribes would be divided into parcels for individual Indian families. In at least one case, it was engineered so that there was more land available than that which was distributed, the balance then sold to white homesteaders. Tens of millions of acres of Indian land was lost by them in these transactions.

Citizenship was granted to landowners under the Act and to any Indians who were willing to give up their tribal life for "civilized" ways. It soon became apparent that this experiment in forcing a new way of life upon the natives was unsuccessful.

It is interesting at this point to look at where the nation was in terms of growth. The following descriptive facts from the year 1909 help us get a better picture of life in U.S.A. at that time for other than the native Indians, so that we can have a better understanding of existing conditions and perhaps better understand what people were thinking at that time rather than trying to look at the situation from our circumstances today.

The average life expectancy was 47 years. Only 14% of the homes had a bathtub and 8% had a telephone. 144 miles of paved roads existed throughout the entire country and a total of 8,000 automobiles. In cities the maximum speed limit was 10 miles an hour.

Workers were paid an average of twenty-two cents an hour, making their annual income somewhere between 200 and 400 dollars a year. Ninety percent of the doctors had no college education. Instead, they attended "medical schools", many of which were considered substandard.

Most women washed their hair once a month and used borax or egg yolks for shampoo. Sugar cost four cents a pound and eggs were fourteen cents a dozen. Coffee was fifteen cents a pound.

The American flag had forty-five stars and the population of Las Vegas, Nevada, a mere thirty people. Two of every ten adults couldn't read or write and only 6% of all Americans were high school graduates. Only 230 murders were reported in the entire country for that year.

In 1934 Congress passed the Indian Reorganization Act, ending the policy of land allotment. It re-established tribes as political entities and reinstated, at least partially, their internal sovereignty and a revival of Indian culture and religion was actually promoted.

Under this new law, many of the tribes set up governments resembling that of the United States. Constitutions were written and adopted which established executive, legislative and judicial branches and provided for elections by secret ballot. There was money in the bill to buy back some of the surplus land which had been lost, along with money for education and medical facilities and an allotment for economic development.

Power was granted which allowed the Indians to remove white men from their land and returned rights to natural resources. Reaction to this reversal was such that in 1955 Congress reversed itself and declared that all federal relations with Indian tribes should be terminated as soon as possible. It also allowed the various states to assume civil and criminal control over the Indian reservations within their boundaries without consent or input from the tribes involved.

Conditions in the United States during the 1960s were turbulent to say the least. Not only was there great disagreement about the Vietnam War, but civil rights activities gained a lot of momentum among many ethnic groups. The Hispanics achieved better wages and improved prestige while the African Americans accomplished tremendous gains as a result of Martin Luther King's non-violent resistance. Even Asians found a reduction in discrimination in the schools.

Earlier, Fortunate Eagle, a resident of the Paiute-Shoshone Reservation in central Nevada had successfully established the United Bay Area Council of American Indian Affairs, Inc. which had created an Indian Center in San Francisco to provide a location where Indians could meet and socialize and help each other. On October 10, 1969, the center burned down.

Several Indian activists then presented the San Francisco City Council with a proposal to turn Alcatraz, which had been abandoned, into an Indian Culture Center. Unfortunately at the same time there was a proposal under consideration involving a plan of Texas millionaire Lamar Hunt to turn Alcatraz into a private commercial venture. With all other options gone with regard to Alcatraz, a plan took form to just go there and stay on the island until the authorities would give it to them for a residence.

More than 6500 Indians took part in the occupation of the facility. They were disenchanted with the failure of the U.S. government to honor treaties and tribal sovereignty. Theirs was an effort to restore the dignity of the more than 540 American Indian nations in the country. Many experts believe that the occupation did, in the long run, improve conditions for the two million plus American and Alaskan Indian descendants of the original inhabitants of this continent.

The people involved were a mixture of college activists, families with children fresh off reservations, and even some who had relocated into cities. All were unhappy with what they considered to be economic, social and political neglect of the Indian population by the United States Government. They believed their effort was about human rights which would be dramatically emphasized by their occupation of Alcatraz.

During the seventeen months of their occupation much had taken place. Conditions on the island were less than ideal. Many who lived there described life as being uncontrolled with numerous factions trying to establish their ideas of how life should be lived. Some saw this as an opportunity to live it up and were constantly partying.

While officials wanted the invaders removed, they feared public opinion. They offered to give them the facilities of Fort Mason in return for their departure.

When their offer was refused, plans for forced removal began to formulate. It was a fire, however, that actually caused the end of the occupation.

Four historical buildings went up in flames. Because they were located at some distance from each other, the Indians believed that government agents had set them, but the government leaders accused rowdy occupiers of starting the fires. Officials increased their demands for the Indians to leave because the island had become a ghetto.

Most did in fact leave and when U.S. Marshals arrived to reclaim the island, only fourteen Indians still remained and they left peacefully.

The U.S. policy of Relocation and Termination had caused many Indians to become restless. Under President Eisenhower the government had initiated the project known as Relocation. It was aimed at encouraging American Indians to leave tribal lands and move into cities where they were promised assistance in getting situated and would be provided with job training. They were given one way bus tickets but no help. They found no housing and were unemployed for many months.

Once again the U.S. government had succeeded in deceiving the Indians. The Bureau of Indian Affairs estimated that between the years of 1952 to 1967 over 200,000 American Indians were lured to cities such as Denver, Chicago, New York, Los Angeles and San Francisco with the promise of a better life, only to find disappointment. By way of contrast, only 89,000 American Indians were removed from their ancestral lands under the Indian Removal Act of 1830.

A survey by Zogby has shown that 88 percent of adults think that the U.S. Government should keep its word and honor the Native American treaties it has made with the nation's Indian tribes in the past.

The executive director of the Native American Finance Officers Association believes that congress should give the tribes the same financing abilities that other governments in the United States enjoy. He claims that when tribes try to finance basic services like water services and reservoirs they are disallowed from using the basic tools of the municipal bond market.

"Conflicting views as to what Congress intended," concludes Desiderio, "are paralyzing the ability of tribes to access the low-cost benefits of tax-exempt financing—the very benefit that was intended for tribes by a Congressional act passed in 1982.

The problem is obviously very complex. While language in the treaties indicate that the Indians have a legal claim to what was once theirs, reality makes it all but impossible to make it happen. It's time that the federal government lived up to its word and made the same tools available to the tribes that every other state and city has. We have asked some of today's Native American Indians what would be a fair resolution from their point of view.

Chapter 10

Comments from Native Americans

In response to a written request for thoughts from the Indians themselves Curtis Yarlott, Executive Director of St. Labre Indian School located in Ashland, Montana, said that what the Indians would like is "education and respect—education for everyone to learn more about each other and respect for each other and our diversities. We may be different in some ways, but we are all 'children of God.'

"We are not two nations. Our country is 'One Nation under God' with many different people. Not just by race or religion, but from one individual to the next. If everyone could respect and accept every other person, the world would be a better place."

In a poem written by a graduate of the Red Cloud Indian School which was founded in 1888 and educates about 600 students annually on the Pine Ridge Indian Reservation in South Dakota, the author dreams of a place where people live in perfect harmony and where color is not wrong.

One can sense the desire for peace, the pain of discriminating remarks and ultimately the longing to be accepted as an equal. In this land of the free, how can such conditions continue to haunt our citizens?

Kevin Yellow Bird Steele of the Wounded Knee District School Foundation in Manderson, SD, offers this Legend of the Dream Catcher in a fund raising pamphlet:

"Long ago when the world was young, an old Lakota spiritual leader was on a high mountain and had a vision.

"In his vision, Iktomi, the great trickster and teacher of wisdom, appeared in the form of a spider.

"Iktomi spoke to him in a sacred language that only the spiritual leader of the Lakota could understand.

"As he spoke, Iktomi (the spider), took the elder's willow hoop which had feathers, horse hair, beads and offerings on it, and began to spin a web. He spoke to the elder about the cycles of life . . . and how we begin our lives as infants and we move on to childhood and then to adult hood. Finally we go to old age where we must be taken care of as infants, completing the cycle.

"'But,' Iktomi said as he continued to spin his web, 'in each time of life there are many forces—some good and some bad. If you listen to the good forces, they will steer you in the right direction. But if you listen to the bad forces, they will hurt you and steer you in the wrong direction.'

"He continued, 'There are many forces and different directions that can help or interfere with the harmony of nature, and also with the Great Spirit and all of his wonderful teachings.'

"All the while the spider spoke, he continued to weave his web starting from the outside and working towards the center.

"When Iktomi finished speaking, he gave the Lakota elder the web and said, 'See the web is a perfect circle but there is a hole in the center of the circle.'

"He said, 'Use the web to help yourself and your people reach your goals and make good use of your people's ideas, dreams and visions.

"'If you believe in the Great Spirit, the web will catch your good ideas—and the bad will go through the hole.'

"The Lakota elder passed on his vision to his people and now the Sioux Indians use the dream catcher as the web of their life.

"It is hung above their beds or in their home to sift their dreams and visions.

"The good in their dreams are captured in the web of life and carried with them . . . but the evil in their dreams escapes through the hole in the center of the web and are no longer a part of them.

"They believe that the dream catcher holds the destiny of their future."

Kevin Yellowbird Steele goes on to say: "You might be surprised to learn what young Indiana children dream of. They don't dream about visiting a lush paradise, being movie stars or becoming rich . . . they dream about things most Americans take for granted, like having food to eat, living in a warm house and graduating from grade school. To an Indian child, his or her dreams are important. In fact, they are life sustaining."

In a fund raising effort Billy Mills head of Running Strong for American Indian Youth, wrote in a letter requesting funds: "your emergency gift can help me continue to provide the life-changing services and desperately needed things such as food, water, clothes, heating fuel and more to remote reservation Indian children and families."

He goes on to describe how the recent recession in this country was "like an earthquake to poor reservations."

Lamenting the reality that the federal government repeatedly broke treaty after treaty and promise after promise, thus breaking faith with American Indian people, he pointed out that Indian reservations were established to 'get rid' of America's 'Indian problem' "Fiercely independent, Indian people were condemned to a confined life on desolate land, oftentimes far from their traditions and sacred homelands. Sacred homelands, the buffalo and, most of all, freedom and independence were stolen from America's first citizens."

Chapter 11

Conclusion

Our machines, technology and systems of managing economic factors offer freedom from back-breaking labor which also produces the opportunity for leisure and some stabilization of nature's cycles. According to our way of thinking, people who live by a never ending search for food and daily provision of their needs would certainly want what we have.

But such is not the situation with the Native American Indians. Yes, they certainly want to be able to survive and to have their daily needs met, but they believe their system of procuring these things is superior to ours and do not want to accept our way of life. They believe that their way of life has served them well for thousands of years and that our way is destructive of the things they hold sacred.

What we find difficult to understand is that Indians are different from us in many ways. We place private property at the top of our list of things that really matter. That includes land but also resources and the ability to buy, sell and inherit. Indians do not believe in private ownership of such resources. They have no concept of owning and selling land, minerals or plant life.

We seek profit and surplus production for sale. The Indians want only subsistence with no profit motive and surplus production sufficient only to provide for possible shortfall. We work long hours, their customary work day is about half of ours.

We regard nature as a resource. The Indians view humans as being part of nature. Most of our decisions are made by executives, by majority vote or by a dictator. Their decisions are usually by a consensus of the whole tribe. We tend to centralize authority, they decentralize it.

Our laws are written and codified. Indian law is passed on orally. We depend upon an adversarial process, they have no adversarial process. Our criminal cases are judged by strangers while theirs are decided by groups of peers.

Our societies are large scale with large populations, theirs is small scale where all people know each other and the population density is low. Our lineage follows the male, theirs the female. We live in small family stature whereas the Indians favor extended families and often many families living together. We revere the young and they revere the old.

Our history is written in books while they pass on historical and other information orally. Memory is extremely important to the Indians, which probably explains why they tend to revere their elders.

We work to develop high technology to change the environment and to control it. The Indians live within the environment and rely on low technology. We haul materials a great distance for construction purposes, they look to the materials that are local. When we build it is for the long haul. The Indians build with the idea that it will revert back to its natural state. We are in love with concrete and cover the land with hard artificial surfaces while the Indians retain the natural surfaces.

Materialism dominates in the Western culture, while for the Indians spirituality is integrated with all aspects of daily life. We tend to work for the future with little reference to yesterday, while the Indians tie together their yesterdays and todays.

Finally, we keep a close watch on the time and measure it meticulously with scientific equipment, such as watches and clocks. For the Indians, time is measured according to the observance of nature and they choose to act when the time is right.

We crimp and save for the future. Sharing and giving is more import for an Indian.

A pamphlet sent from Father Emmett Hoffman, founder of Soaring Eagle, a Public Charity in Billings, Montana, gives us a good look at what the Cheyenne believe. Entitled, "Journey of Life," it features on its cover the symbol known as the Morning Star which is the official emblem of the Northern Cheyenne tribe. It represents the sacred wisdom of the past and the power that will guide them into the future.

"Morning Star was the name given to Chief Dull Knife who reigned over a hundred years ago who led his followers into their home in Montana. The Morning Star has "inspired, guided and united us as a tribe in the spirit of hope."

The pamphlet describes that in Native American tradition the seasons are linked to the four cardinal directions. East is Spring and represents creation or birth which is symbolized by the color of white for purity. South is the summer and symbolizes the child who reaches adolescence and becomes educated. It is represented by the color red which stands for growth.

West is the fall and produces maturity. The adult follows the right path and achieves respect and honor. The color of yellow signifies fulfillment. North is winter and the adult moves into the status of the elders where knowledge leads to wisdom. It represents completion and is symbolized by the color black.

Another Cheyenne chief, Highchief, is quoted in the pamphlet and describes the era when contact with the white man changed forever the way of life for the Native Americans.

"Once, only Indians lived in this land. Then came strangers from across the Great Water. No land had they, we gave them our land. No food had they; we gave them of our corn. The strangers are becoming many and they fill all the country. They dig gold from my mountains; they build houses of the trees of my forests; they rear cities of my stones and rocks; they make fine garments from the hides of animals that eat my grass. None of the things that make their riches did they bring with them from beyond the Great Water; all comes from my land, the land the Great Mystery gave unto the Indian.

"And when I think upon this, I know it is right, even this. In the heart of the Great Mystery it was meant that strangers/visitors—my friends across the Great Water—should come to my land; that I should bid them welcome; that all men should sit down with me and eat together of my corn. It was meant by the Great Mystery that the Indian should give to all people."

The Cheyenne weathered many hard times in spite of their traditional culture being pushed aside. They continue to struggle looking for a chance for regeneration and renewal.

These cultural differences find expression in ways of life that are in sharp contrast with each other. They impose difficulty in understanding the whys and wherefores that transpire when the two interact.

And probably the most difficult thing for either to understand is why the other person can't understand their point of view.

Under any circumstances, the present plight of these descendants of the original inhabitants of this land is unconscionable and we have an inherited responsibility for what our ancestors did to them. At the very least, we should want to offer whatever financial assistance we can to improve their existing living conditions and to assist in providing education which is the basis for their self-improvement and also to seek ways that will improve their opportunities to become self-sufficient in our modern society.

We should also respect their culture and recognize their right to live under their own religious beliefs. We should extend to them, as equals, the Constitutional rights that we enjoy.

We hear a great deal about outsourcing manufacturing jobs and in fact, we produce very little in America today, while once we were the leaders in manufacturing of just about everything. Our ability to produce goods was one of the leading reasons we were able to tool up for war after Pearl Harbor. Today it is hard to find products with labels that indicate they were made in the USA.

We are told that we need to have illegal workers to do the tasks that our people do not want to do. It would seem that doing some of these tasks would be better than starving to death or living in the conditions which exist on Indian reservations.

We also know that taxes in this country cause a major problem for our corporations, making it more economical to have the work done in foreign countries. Is it possible that tax advantages might be negotiated for building plants on reservations in Indian nations to alleviate unemployment?

Some Indian reservations are located so remotely from where jobs exist that they can't get to work. Food stamps prove ineffective because there are no stores in which to redeem them. The mechanics of providing relief over the vast distances and poor highways are obstacles that add immeasurably to the costs of supplying emergency assistance. In many locations the soil is so poor that agriculture is difficult, if not impossible.

We have knowledge that could overcome all of these obstacles and put in place systems that would provide employment. We could relax some of the restrictions that currently prevent Native Americans from accessing minerals, fish and other natural resources.

The United States has expended a great deal of money to relieve urban city poverty, but has not exercised the innate innovation that has made our country great with regard to the Native Americans. We need to focus on the problem and find answers. We have put these individuals in situations where they depend upon the government and once again it has failed to perform. It is time to keep the promises made by our past generations for the collective moral health of our entire nation. Some decisions made in the past need to be reversed or modified. But what is needed is action rather than words.

Bibliography

"We've Done Them Wrong"

* "This Day in North American Indian History" by Phil Konstantin
* Federally Recognized Native American Indian Tribes
* "American Holocast: Columbus and the Conquest of the New World" (Oxford University Press, 1992) by David E. Stannard
* Remarks of Kevin Gover, Assistant Secretary for Indian Affairs, Department of the Interior at the Ceremony of the 175th Anniversary of the Establishment of the Bureau of Indian Affairs. September 8, 2000
* Age of Discovery: mhtml:file://C:/Documents and Settings
* Native Americans: http://history-world.org/american_indians-or-native_ameri.
* Native Americans in the United States: http://en.wikipedia.org/wiki/Native_ Americans_in_the_United-States
* Walum Olum: http://en.wikipedia.org/Wlaum_Olum
* "First People: The Early Indians of Virginia" by Keith Egloff &Deborah Woodward
* "The Seed of a Nation" by Darrell fields
* Frame of Government, William Penn. http//www.constitution.org.bep/frompenn
* Charter of Privileges; www.constitution.org.bep/penncharpriv.htm **
* American Indian Horse History: http//www.indianhorse.com
* "America's Fascinating Indian Heritage": The Reader's Digest Assoc., Inc.
* "Cherokee People of the World" by Wayne L. Youngblood
* "In the Absence of the Sacred" by Jerry Mander
* Who was Who in Native American History

* National Congress of American Indians: History: http://www.ncai.org/?8
* The Great Law of Peace: http://iroquoisdemocracy.pdx.edu/htm/activity4.htm
* The Spanish Conquest of Native America http://www.floridahistory.com
* The History of Jamestown: http://en.wikipedia.org/wiki/JamestownVirginia
* British Colonization of the Americas: http://wikipedia.org
* The New York Times: Wednesday, January 27, 2010 Archives
* Amnesty Magazine: "Soul Wound; the Legacy of Native American Indians" by Andrea Smith
* Indian Removal Act: Summary, Facts, Native American History essays
* Walter Breen's complete Encyclopedia of U.S. and Canadian Coins
* "Money for Indian Scalps: The New York Times, Published: Oct. 12, 1885
* History of American Indian Boarding Schools: http//kporterfield.com/aicttw/articles/boardingschool.html
* The 1810 Massacre of 110 Cherokee Women and Children at Yahoo Falls, Kentucky, http://Victorian.fortunecity.com/Rothko/420/amyuntikwataski/yahoo

* Statutes of the United States Concerning Native Americans: http://Avalon.law.edu/subject_menus/namenu.asp
  The Indian Removal Act of 1830 http://www.civics-online.org/library/formatted/texxtx/indian_act.html
* Indian Removal Act: summary, Facts, Andrew Jackson http://ashevillelist.com/history/indian-removal.htm
* Indian Wars Time Table: http://www.u-s-history.com/pages/h1008.html

* Native American Atrocities: Wind Wolf Woman
* American Indians Contribution to the World: http://www.kporterfield.com
* Charles Eastman: http://www.answers.com
* James Thorpe: http://angelfire.comcrazy3/nyashia/western/index.blog?topic
* Billy Mills: http://www.indianyouth.org/billymills.html
* Will Rogers: http://www.cmgww.com/historic/rogers/biography.htm
* John Harrington: http://www.jsc.nasa.gpv/Bios/htmlbios/herringt.html

* Navajo Code Talkers: http://www.archives.gov/publications/ prologue/2001
* Native American and the U.S. Military: http://history.navy.mil/ faqs/faq61-1.htm
* Lewis and Clark: Native American Contributions: http// nationalgeographic.com
* "California History: The Hidden Genocide," by Norma Jean Croy
* "Alcatraz, Indian Land" b y Ben Winton Native Peoples Magazine Fall 1999
* Oregon Coast Magazine Online: Travel and History
* Bureau of Indian Affairs Web Site; http://www.bia.gov/WhatWeDo/ index.htm
* U.S History Encyclopedia: Indian Agents*
* The Intelligencer, Friday, Dec. 4, 2009: IRS Sells Indian Tribe Land to Settle Debt
* Federal Government Swindles Native Americans Again—John Ransom, Townhall Magazine, 11/16/11
  * Great Falls Tribune, June 23,2002
  * Everett Herald, July11,2002
  * Rocky Mountain News, September 12,2002
  * Denver Post August 18,2003
  * Indian Country Today, March 10,2004
  * Pamphlets: Soaring Eagle, A Public Charity: Billings MN 59103
    Oglala Lakota College: Kyle, SD 57752
    Wounded Knee District School Foundation: Manderson, SD 57756
    St. Labre Indian School: Ashland Montana 59004
    Southwest Indian Relief Council: Mesa, AZ 5211
    Native American Aid: Spearfish, SD 57783
    Sioux Nation Relief Fund, Albert Lea, MN 56007-9841

Native American Charities

American Indian Relief Council: Darwin Long, PO Box 6200 Rapid City, SD 57709-6200

American Indian Education Foundation, A Program of National Relief Charities: Paula Long Fox, PO Box 6041 Albert Lea, MN 56007-9840

Catholic Indian Mission, Fr. Basil Atwell, OSB, Standing Rock Indian Reservation PO Box 639 Fort Yates ND 58538-0639

Council of Indian Nations: Lovena B. Lee, PO Box 1800 Apache Junction, AZ 85217

Native American Aid: Linwood TallBull, PO Box 5500 Spearfish, SD 57783

Native American Children Fund: W.T.Jeffers, World Changers Int'l Ministries PO Box 25 Sapulpa, OK 74067

National American Emergency Relief %World Emergency Processing Center: PO Box 52051 Phoenix, AZ 85072-2051

Navajo Relief Fund, National Relief Charities: PO Box 90000 Flagstaff, AZ 86003-9927

Oglala Lakota College: Thomas Shortbull Pres. PO Box 537 Kyle, SD 57752-0537

Red Cloud Indian School: Father Peter Klink S.J., Pine Ridge SD 57770

Running Strong for American Indian Youth: Billy Mills 2550 Huntington Ave. Ste200 Alexandria, VA 22303-1499

Sioux Nation Relief Fund, A Program of National Relief Charities: Marion A. One Star, PO Box 5092 Sioux Falls, SD 57117-9867

Soaring Eagle: Father Emmett Hoffman, 745 Indian Trail PO Drawer 879 Billings, MT 59103

Southwest Indian Relief Council: Katie Tree PO Box 16777 Mesa, AZ 85211

St. Bonaventure Indian Mission & School: Christopher Halter, PO Box 9527 Wilson, NH 03086-9527

St. Joseph's Indian School, PO Box 300 Chamberlain, SD 57325-0300

St. Labre Indian School: Curtis Yarlott Ashland, Montana 59004

Wounded Knee District School Foundation: Kevin Yellow Bird Steele 100 School Rd. Manderson, SD 57756